CYCLE 4

5e

Nouveau programme

What's on...

WORKBOOK

A1 A2

Sous la direction de
James WINDSOR
IA-IPR Académie de Bordeaux

Sandrine CHAHED
Professeur certifié
Collège Aliénor d'Aquitaine, Bordeaux (33)

Laurence GIAMMATTEI
Professeur certifié
Collège Jules Ferry, Langon (33)

Catherine HOOPER
Professeur certifié hors classe
Collège Jules Ferry, Langon (33)

hachette
ÉDUCATION
vous accompagne

Bienvenue dans *workbook*
What's on... 5e !

Grâce à la collection *What's on...*, tu vas enfin pouvoir apprendre l'anglais :

- **à ton propre rythme** puisque **deux questionnements** te sont proposés dans ton *workbook* pour chacun des documents que tu vas étudier avec ton professeur en classe ;
- **en étant acteur de ton apprentissage** puisque tu vas choisir le questionnement, A ou B, le mieux adapté à ta compréhension et/ou à ta perception du document, et cela sans aucun jugement sur ton niveau d'anglais ;
- **en bénéficiant de conseils dans ta découverte de cette langue étrangère** pour te permettre d'aborder de manière méthodique tout document, écrit ou oral ;
- **en enrichissant ton vocabulaire** grâce à des boîtes d'aide et à des exercices ludiques sur le thème de la séquence abordée en classe, à la fin du *workbook* ;
- **en perfectionnant ta grammaire et ta prononciation** à l'aide d'exercices te permettant notamment de comprendre les mécanismes de l'anglais ;
- **en t'auto-évaluant pour constater que le travail réalisé t'a permis de progresser.**

***What's on...* : à toi de le découvrir !**

Les auteurs

Couverture : Anne-Danielle Naname
Mise en page : Anne-Danielle Naname – Laurine Caucat
Illustrations : Céline Pesle
Recherche iconographique : Laetitia Guillemin
Relecture ortho-typographique : Yoko Lacour
Édition : Dorothée Rouffiac et Jeanne Digne-Matz

www.hachette-education.com

ISBN : 978-2-01-462724-4

Sommaire

1 Let's talk about school

1 First day blues

GET READY!

→ Book p. 18

Look and react

1. What sort of document is it?

a. It is...
- [ ] a cartoon.
- [x] a frame from a comic strip.
- [ ] a photo.

b. Who is the comic book illustrator?
- [ ] Peter M. Schulz.
- [x] Charles M. Schulz.
- [ ] Charlie Schulz.

c. Where does it take place?
- [ ] At school.
- [ ] In a kitchen.
- [x] In a bedroom.

2. Who can you see?

I can see...
- [ ] two boys.
- [x] a boy and a girl.
- [ ] a boy and a dog.

3. What day is it?

a. It is...
- [x] the first day of school.
- [ ] the last day of school.
- [ ] the summer holidays.

b. The girl is certainly...
- [ ] happy.
- [x] nervous.
- [ ] sad.

c. The boy is...
- [x] surprised.
- [ ] hungry.
- [ ] excited.

GO! VIDEO 1 → Book p. 18

Comment on the video. Choose between the following exercises (A or B).

ACCOMPAGNEMENT PERSONNALISÉ AP

DIFFÉRENCIATION

CONSEILS

- Tu vas regarder la vidéo trois fois.
- Regarde bien les images pour repérer les lieux.
- Concentre-toi sur les mots que tu connais déjà.

A

First viewing

a. The video is about...

- [ ] a girl going to Primary school for the first time.
- [x] a girl going to Middle school for the first time.
- [ ] a girl going to University for the first time.

b. How old are the pupils going to Middle School?

In the USA, they are aged from...

- [ ] 5 to 11 years old.
- [ ] 15 to 18 years old.
- [x] 11 to 15 years old.

Second viewing

c. What are her feelings?

She feels...

- [ ] happy and excited.
- [x] scared and nervous.
- [ ] curious and talkative.

d. For her first period/class she feels...

- [x] lonely.
- [ ] calm.
- [ ] bored.

e. Because...

- [x] she can't see her friends.
- [ ] the lesson is too long.
- [ ] there are only boys in her class.

f. She hopes that her friends...

- [ ] are okay.
- [x] are going to be in her classes.
- [ ] are not lost.

Third viewing

g. What question are the other pupils asked?

- [x] How they feel for this first day at Middle school.
- [ ] If the cafeteria is good.
- [ ] If the teachers are nice.

h. The other pupils feel...

- [x] scared.
- [x] afraid.
- [ ] quiet.
- [x] nervous.
- [x] shy.
- [x] lost.
- [ ] patient.

B

CONSEILS

- Lis attentivement chaque question et les choix de réponses avant d'y répondre.
- Lors de la mise en commun, écoute bien les réponses et n'hésite pas à participer.
- À la maison, relis attentivement tes notes et mémorise les nouveaux mots et expressions.

First viewing

a. What is the video about?

The video is about ..... a girl ..... going for the first time to ..... Middle school/Junior school ..... in the ..... USA .....

b. What is the name of her school?

It is... [ ] Township Junior High. [x] Townsend Junior High. [ ] Townsend Senior High.

c. How old are the pupils in this type of school?

In the USA, they are aged from ..... 11 ..... to ..... 15 years old ......

Second viewing

d. What are her feelings?

She feels...

- [ ] happy and excited.
- [x] scared and nervous.
- [ ] curious and talkative.

e. Because it is a very...

- [x] nervous and thrilling moment for a kid.
- [ ] hilarious and important moment for a kid.

f. For her first period/class she feels nervous and lonely because...

- [x] she can't see her friends.
- [ ] the lesson is too long.
- [ ] there are only boys in her class.

g. She hopes that her friends...

- [ ] are okay.
- [x] are going to be in her classes.
- [ ] are not lost.

Vocabulary

- **fra**me
- shy
- **sca**red
- af**raid**
- **thril**ling
- **lon**ely
- if
- hope

Third viewing

h. What question are the other pupils asked?

They are asked: "How did ......you feel when you entered the school......?"

i. It means...

- [x] how they feel on their first day at school.
- [ ] what they think about their new school.
- [ ] what they think about their new teachers.

j. Their answer:

They feel...

- [x] scared.
- [x] afraid.
- [ ] quiet.
- [x] nervous.
- [x] shy.
- [x] lost.
- [ ] patient.

2 My ideal school

GET READY!

→ Book p. 19

Look at the document and answer the questions below.

1. What can you say about this document?

It is about… ☐ a school in the UK. ☑ important things in an ideal school. ☐ a description of your school.

2. What are the important elements in an ideal school?

- ☑ Teachers.
- ☑ Rules.
- ☑ Subjects.
- ☐ Swimming-pool.
- ☑ After school activities.
- ☑ Playground.
- ☐ Uniform.
- ☑ Facilities.

GO!

→ Book p. 19

Read the text on the next page.

CONSEILS

- Lis le texte au moins deux fois.
- Avant de commencer, souligne les mots que tu connais déjà
- et entoure ceux que tu ne connais pas.

2 My ideal school

My ideal school
Man Tsz Ho, Macro (Hong-Kong)

My ideal school is in the countryside[1]. The students don't need to wear uniform. There are many school facilities. It has a five-storey[2] building with a sport court. On the ground floor, there are a playground, a canteen and a hall. There are many special rooms on the first floor. There are a library, two computer rooms, an art room, a music room and a classroom. There are ten classrooms and two toilets on each floor. In the sport court, there are two changing rooms, two toilets, two basketball courts, four badminton courts and a football ground.

Adapted from: www.clementi.edu.hk

1. campagne - 2. de cinq étages

Choose between the following exercises (A or B).

AP ACCOMPAGNEMENT PERSONNALISÉ

DIFFÉRENCIATION

A

First reading

a. What is the text about? Give the title of the document: My ideal school

b. Where is this school situated? [ ] In the city. [x] In the countryside. [ ] On an island.

c. How many floors are there in the school? [ ] 2 [ ] 4 [x] 5

Justify your answer by quoting the text: "It has a five-storey building".

Second reading

d. Talk about the facilities in this ideal school. How many classrooms are there on each floor? [ ] 2 [ ] 6 [x] 10

e. What facilities are there in the sport court?

- [x] Toilets.
- [ ] Three changing rooms.
- [x] Two basketball courts.
- [ ] Two tennis courts.
- [ ] A rugby ground.
- [x] A football ground.

f. Are there changing rooms? [x] Yes, there are. [ ] No, there are not.

g. What about the facilities for artistic activities?

There are a music room and an art room.

Third reading

h. What can you do in this ideal school?

- [x] Work with computers.
- [x] Go to the library.
- [ ] Dance.
- [x] Play music.
- [ ] Go to the swimming-pool.
- [x] Have lunch at the canteen.
- [x] Practise sports.
- [ ] Play rugby.

i. Can you play badminton? Justify your answer. ☑ Yes, I can. ☐ No, I can't.

I can play badminton because there are four badminton courts.

j. Complete the sentence. Use the answers above.

In this ideal school, I can work with computers in computer rooms, go to the library, play music in the music room, practise sports and have lunch at the canteen.

k. What about a school uniform?

☑ I don't need one. ☐ There is a school uniform for pupils.

l. What do you think of this ideal school?

☑ I think my school is really an ideal school.
☐ I think it is a boring place.
☐ My school is already an ideal school!

CONSEILS

- Pour t'aider, tu peux faire un schéma de l'école après avoir lu le texte.
- Après la correction des activités, relis le texte et fais une liste des mots que tu comprends désormais.

B

First reading

a. What is the text about? Give its title.

The title of the document is *My ideal school*.

b. Whose ideal school is it? It is Mao Tzs Ho's ideal school.

c. Where is this school situated?

It is situated in the countryside.

d. How many floors are there in the school? Justify your answer by quoting the text.

There are 5 floors in this school.

"It has a five-storey building."

Second reading

e. Talk about the facilities. How many classrooms are there on each floor?

There are 10 classrooms on each floor.

f. What facilities are there in the sport court?

There are toilets, two changing rooms, two basketball courts, a football ground and four badminton courts.

g. Are there any changing rooms?

Yes, there are two changing rooms in the sport court.

h. Talk about the facilities for artistic activities.

There are a music room and an art room.

Vocabulary

- floor
- ground
- court
- **chang**ing-room
- **li**brary
- **class**room

Third reading

i. Say what you can do in this ideal school.

In this ideal school, I can work with computers in computer rooms, go to the library, play music in the music room, practise sports and have lunch at the canteen.

j. What about a school uniform?

I don't need a uniform, I can wear casual clothes.

k. Can you go to the swimming-pool in this school?

No, I can't because there is no swimming-pool.

l. What do you think of this ideal school? What about your school?

I think this school is really an ideal school!

My school is already an ideal school!

I hope my school is going to be an ideal school.

PREPARE YOUR FINAL TASKS

→ Book p. 19

Using the text, prepare some ideas about your ideal school (facilities, activities...).

My ideal school is situated ...

There is a ... and there is a ...

There are ...

It has ... and ...

In my ideal school I can ...

Pupils can ...

CONSEILS

- Tu peux utiliser le texte de la leçon pour guider ta présentation.
- Tu peux aussi utiliser ton workbook et tes notes pour t'aider.
- Entraîne-toi à prendre la parole avec 5 ou 6 mots-clefs sous les yeux.

3 School in Great Britain

GET READY!

→ Book p. 20

Look at the document and answer the questions below.

1. **What sort of document is it?**
   - ☐ It is a video.
   - ☐ It is a photograph.
   - ☑ It is a chart.

2. **Name the two schools systems mentioned in the document.**
   - ☑ The French school system.
   - ☑ The British school system.
   - ☐ The American school system.

Comparison of school systems

British	
Infant School Key stage 1	Year 1 / Year 2
Junior / Primary School Key stage 2	Year 2 / Year 3
	Year 3 / Year 4
	Year 4 / Year 5
	Year 5 / Year 6
Secondary School Key stage 3	Year 6 / Year 7
	Year 7 / Year 8
	Year 8 / Year 9
Key stage 4	Year 9 / Year 10
	Year 10 / Year 11
Sixth form	Year 11 / Year 12
	Year 12 / Year 13

French	
Élémentaire	CP (6 ans)
	CE1
	CE2
	CM1
	CM2
Collège	6e
	5e
	4e
	3e
Lycée	2nde
	1ère
	Terminale

P011-2-9782014627244
P011-4-9782014627244
un peu trop sombre

GO!

→ Book p. 20

Read and comment on the text.

www.afternoonlessonsinUK.com

Afternoon Lessons

Lessons resume[1] with reading activities. This could be the whole class quietly reading or the children undertaking[2] various reading activities in groups. The rest of the afternoon is spent learning one or two of our other school subjects. The photos opposite are examples of some of the lessons the children may learn.

Afternoon lessons continue until **3:15 pm** when the children go home. There are many different clubs and activities for the children to join.

Art

Music

Science

Geography

1. reprennent – 2. effectuant

School in Great Britain

ACCOMPAGNEMENT PERSONNALISÉ AP

DIFFÉRENCIATION

Choose between the following exercises (A or B).

A

First reading

a. What type of document is it?

It is...

- [x] a screenshot from a website.
- [ ] an article.
- [ ] a photograph.

b. It is...

- [ ] a university website.
- [x] a school website.
- [ ] a shopping website.

Second reading

c. It is about...

- [ ] morning lessons.
- [x] afternoon lessons.
- [ ] evening lessons.

d. Give information about the lessons. What do the pupils do first in the afternoon?

- [ ] They sleep.
- [ ] They write.
- [x] They read.

e. How many school subjects do they study in the afternoon?

- [x] 1 or 2.
- [ ] 2 or 3.
- [ ] 3 or 4.

Third reading

f. Look at the pictures and describe the different afternoon activities. What are their names?

Art, Science, Music and Geography.

g. What time do children finish school?

- [ ] At quarter to three pm.
- [x] At quarter past three pm.
- [ ] At quarter past three am.

h. After school, children...

- [x] go home.
- [x] join clubs or activities.
- [ ] do after school jobs.

CONSEILS

- Lis le texte trois fois. Concentre-toi
- sur les mots que tu connais déjà.
- Aide-toi des images et des mots
- transparents ou quasi-transparents.

B

First reading

a. What type of document is it?

It is... [x] a screenshot from a website. [ ] an article. [ ] a photograph.

b. What sort of website is it? It is a school website.

Second reading

c. What is it about? It is about afternoon lessons at a school.

d. What do the pupils do first in the afternoon? First, they read.

e. How many school subjects do they study in the afternoon?

They study 1 or 2 school subjects in the afternoon.

Third reading

f. What time do children finish school? They finish school at quarter past three pm.

g. What do the children do after school? They go home or they join clubs or activities.

h. Name the different afternoon activities they can do.

Art, Science, Music, Geography

CONSEILS

- Mémorise les noms des matières scolaires en anglais, cela te sera utile pour les tâches finales.
- À la maison, relis attentivement tes notes, puis écris les mots-clefs de la leçon avant de les mémoriser.

Vocabulary

- **screen**shot
- a chart
- crafts
- join
- **stud**y

4 School reports

GET READY! → Book p. 21

1. doit être – 2. un bon à rien

Look at the document and answer the questions.

1. What sort of document is it?

a. It is...
- [x] a cartoon/a funny drawing.
- [ ] a movie.
- [ ] a photo.

b. Who is the cartoonist?

It is...
- [ ] Peter Wilkinson.
- [x] Peter Nicholson.
- [ ] Peter Wicholson.

2. Who can you see?

I can see...
- [ ] a mother, a father and their son.
- [x] a teacher, a father and his son.
- [ ] a teacher, a mother and her son.

3. Describe the situation.

a. The teacher is...
- [ ] giving the father his boy's school report.
- [ ] speaking about the boy's good results at school.
- [x] making nasty comments about the boy's results.

b. What is the father's reaction?

- At first, the father looks... [x] angry [ ] happy [ ] reserved because for him a school report must be... [ ] simple and direct. [x] clear and honest. [ ] long and complicated.
- And then, he looks... [ ] tired [x] demoralized [ ] satisfied because he knows the teacher is... [x] right. [ ] wrong about his son and himself.

c. What about the son?

☐ He looks indifferent. ☑ He feels sorry and embarassed for his father. ☐ He is laughing.

d. Is there irony in this cartoon?

☑ Yes, there is. ☐ No, there isn't.

GO! → Book p. 21

Read and comment on the text.

CONSEILS

- Tu vas lire le document plusieurs fois. Repère les mots que tu connais déjà.

Ash Tree Learning Center Academy
2512 Habersham Street
Savannah, GA 31401

Student:
Felicity Bradshaw*481 First Ave.,
10016 New York, NY, United States

Grade: 7th Grade
Term: Term 2 2015/2016

Subject	Qtr 1		Qtr 2		Sem 1		Qtr 3		Qtr 4		Sem 2		Final	
Art	A	95	A–	92	A	93.5	A–	92	A+	100	A	96	A	94.75
History	A–	90	A	93	A–	91.5	A–	92	A–	92	A–	92	A–	91.75
Language Arts	B+	89	A–	90	A–	89.5	A–	90	B+	88	A	92.5	A–	91
Mathematics	A–	91	A–	91	A–	91	A–	92	A–	92	A–	92	A–	91.5
Science	A	96	A	95	A	95.5	A	94	A	94	A	94	A	94.75
Spanish	A	93	A	93	A	93	A	95	A–	92	A	93.5	A	93.25
Technology	A–	92	A	94	A	93	A+	98	A	95	A+	96.5	A	94.75
				GPA	**3.81**		**4.00**		**4.00**		**4.04**		**3.87**	

Scale: 97-100 = A+ | 93-96 = A | 90-92 = A– | 87-89 = B+ | 83-86 = B | 80-82 = B– | 77-79 = C+ | 73-76 = C | 70-72 = C– | 63-66 = D | 67-69 = D+ | 60-62 = D– | 0-59 = F

Choose between the following exercises (A or B).

AP ACCOMPAGNEMENT PERSONNALISÉ

DIFFÉRENCIATION

A

First reading

a. What sort of document is it? The document is...

☐ a test. ☑ a school report (UK)/a report card (US). ☐ the results of a poll.

b. Whose report is it? It is... ☐ Felicity Huffman's. ☐ Felicity Bradshown's. ☑ Felicity Bradshaw's.

c. What year is she in? She is in... ☐ 5th grade. ☐ 9th grade. ☑ 7th grade.

d. What school is it?

☑ Ash Tree Learning Center Academy. ☐ Anna Middle School. ☐ Poplar Tree Academy.

Second reading

e. How many subjects does this pupil study? This pupil studies...
☐ 5 subjects. ☐ 8 subjects. ☑ 7 subjects.

f. She studies...
☐ French, English and Maths. ☑ Spanish, Maths, History, Science, Technology, Art and Language Arts.

Third reading

g. Talk about her results. She has got a lot of... ☑ A 's ☐ B's ☐ C's ☐ D's

h. What is her final GPA (Grade point average)?
It is... ☐ 4.00 ☐ 3.81 ☑ 3.87

i. I think she has...
☑ good results at school. ☐ bad results at school.

B

First reading

a. What sort of document is it? It is a school report.

b. Whose report is it? It is Felicity Bradshaw's school report.

c. What year is she in? She is in 7th grade.

d. What school is it? It is Ash Tree Learning Center Academy.

Second reading

e. How many subjects does she study? She studies 7 subjects.

f. What subjects does she study?

She studies Spanish, Maths, History, Science, Technology, Art and Language Arts.

Third reading

g. Talk about her results. She has got a lot of A's.

h. What is her final GPA (Grade point average)? It is 3.87.

i. I think she has good results at school.

CONSEILS

Avant de répondre aux questions, prends le temps de bien lire plusieurs fois le document. Aide-toi des mots que tu connais, des couleurs et des éléments en gras pour guider ta lecture.

Vocabulary

- a poll
- **grad**e point average
- **nas**ty
- a re**port** card
- **grad**e
- re**sul**ts

4 School reports

PREPARE YOUR FINAL TASKS

→ Book p. 21

Get in groups and discuss school reports in France. Are they identical or different from the American ones? Which system do you prefer?

I think that in France... / French reports are... / In the UK, the reports are...

CONSEILS

- Discute avec tes camarades. Fais une liste des points communs et des différences entre les bulletins. Quels sont les avantages et les inconvénients de chaque système ? Quel système préfères-tu ?

5 School uniform

GET READY!

→ Book p. 22

Look at the document and answer the questions.

1. What can you see?

- ☐ People in a restaurant.
- ☐ People at work.
- ☑ Teenagers at school.

2. What clothes are they wearing and why?

a. Match the pictures and the words.

a tie • a shirt • a school uniform • a blazer • a coat • shoes • a school badge • a skirt

b. They are wearing ......a school uniform...... because...
- ☐ they want to look identical.
- ☐ they think it is fashionable.
- ☑ they must wear uniforms in British schools.

GO! → Book p. 22

Read and comment on the texts.

CONSEILS

- Tu vas lire les deux textes au moins trois fois.
- Repère les mots concernant les vêtements que tu connais déjà.
- Souligne les mots difficiles.
- Ne t'inquiète pas si tu ne comprends pas tous les mots. Les exercices vont t'aider à mieux comprendre.

CORRECT UNIFORM:

✔

Sharples School uniform is compulsory and should be worn correctly at all times.

- **Blazer:** graphite grey with school badge.
- **Shirt:** white with buttoned collar.
- **Tie:** standard striped tie with school badge visible.
- **Trousers:** black, formal.
- **Skirt:** black, formal, no shorter than one inch above the knee.
- **Socks:** black or white.
- **Shoes:** black leather or simulated leather. Black laces.
- **Coat:** plain, no denim, no leather, no hoodies.

INCORRECT UNIFORM:

✘

- Shirt collar unbuttoned.
- Tie loose and knotted incorrectly.
- Skirt pulled up more than one inch above the knee.
- No boots or trainer-style shoes.
- Make-up, jewellery and nail varnish must not be worn. No piercings allowed.
- Mobile phones must not be placed in pockets and will be confiscated if visible.

5 School uniform

Choose between the following exercises (A or B).

AP — ACCOMPAGNEMENT PERSONNALISÉ — DIFFÉRENCIATION

A

First reading

a. What can you see on this document?

- [ ] An article in a newspaper.
- [x] Sharples School uniform policy.
- [ ] Photos for a clothes shop.

b. What is in the incorrect uniform? Tick the correct answers.

- [ ] Blazer
- [x] Boots
- [x] Make-up
- [ ] Shirt
- [ ] Tie
- [x] Piercing
- [x] Nail varnish
- [x] Leather
- [ ] Collar

c. Write the opposite words face to face: relaxed – unbuttoned – loose – knotted – invisible – buttoned – correctly – visible – plain – elaborate – formal – incorrectly

buttoned – unbuttoned | plain – elaborate

invisible – visible | loose – knotted

correctly – incorrectly | formal – relaxed

Second reading

d. Read the text about the correct uniform and give the colour associated to each clothes.

Blazers: graphite grey — Trousers: black — Socks: black or white

Shirt: white — Skirt: black — Shoes: black

Third reading

e. Right or wrong? Justify your answer.

At Sharples School, pupils must wear a uniform. Right: "school uniform is compulsory".

They must wear a school badge. Right: "With school badge visible".

They must not wear a buttoned shirt collar. Wrong: "shirt with buttoned collar".

They must wear piercings or a stud. Wrong: "No piercing allowed".

Girls must wear a long skirt. Right: "No shorter than one inch above the knee".

They must keep their phones in their pockets. Wrong: "Phones must not be placed in pockets".

Phones will be confiscated if visible. Right: "Will be confiscated if visible".

f. Write a few lines to say what is correct or incorrect at Sharples School. Start your sentences with "They must..." or "They must not..." and use some of the following words:
black or white socks – a school badge – make-up – piercings – plain coat – boots – jewellery.

They must wear black or white socks, they must wear a school badge and they mustn't wear make-up, jewellery or piercings.

B

First reading

a. What can you see?

It's a document on a school uniform.

b. Find the name of the school.

The name of the school is Sharples School.

CONSEILS

- Lis attentivement le document.
- Associe mentalement chacune des phrases au vêtement qui lui correspond sur l'image.
- Essaie de reformuler les obligations et les interdictions vestimentaires de cette école.

Vocabulary

- a school **ba**dge
- a skirt
- **po**licy
- nail **var**nish
- **fa**shionable
- com**pul**sory

c. What is in the incorrect uniform?
Tick the correct answers.

- [ ] blazer
- [x] boots
- [x] make-up
- [ ] shirt
- [ ] tie
- [x] piercing
- [x] nail varnish
- [x] leather
- [ ] collar

d. Find the opposite words in the texts: invisible – relaxed – unbuttonned – knotted/tied – incorrectly – elaborate.

visible – formal – buttoned – loose – correctly – plain.

Second reading

e. Read the text about the correct uniform. Give the colour associated to each clothes.

Socks must be black or white.

Shirts must be white.

Shoes must be black.

Trousers must be black.

Blazers must be graphite grey.

f. Now say what colours pupils must wear.

They must wear a graphite grey blazer, a white shirt, a striped tie, black trousers, a black skirt, black or white socks, black shoes and a plain coat.

g. Finish the sentences and associate the clothes with the correct adjectives.

Shirt collars must be buttoned. Phones must not be visible

Ties must be knotted, not loose. Ties must be striped.

Coats must be plain.

Third reading

h. Write a few lines to say what is correct or incorrect at Sharples School. Start your sentences with "They must..." or "They must not..." and use some of the following words:
black or white socks – a school badge – make-up – piercings – plain coat – black rucksacks – striped tie – boots.

They must wear black or white socks, they must wear a school badge and they mustn't wear make-up, jewellery or piercings.

6 Wrong shoes

GET READY!

→ Book p. 23

Look at the photo and answer the questions.

1. Who can you see?

- [x] A teenage girl.
- [ ] A teenage boy.
- [ ] An adult.

2. What does she have in her hands?

- [ ] A pair of black high heels.
- [x] Black "runners"/trainers.
- [ ] Black boots.

3. How does she look?

She looks...

- [ ] happy.
- [ ] sad.
- [x] upset.

GO!

VIDEO 2

→ Book p. 23

Watch the video and comment. Choose between the following exercises (A or B).

AP ACCOMPAGNEMENT PERSONNALISÉ

DIFFÉRENCIATION

CONSEILS

Regarde la vidéo trois fois.
Sois attentif à ce que disent Riley et sa mère. Note les termes que tu ne comprends pas.

A

First viewing

a. What can you say about this document?

- [x] It is a video.
- [ ] It is an article.
- [ ] It is a photograph.

b. Riley is...

- [x] a schoolgirl at a local school.
- [ ] a student at a local university.

c. This video is about...

- [ ] school and uniforms.
- [ ] school and food.
- [x] school and shoes.

Second viewing

d. What is the problem?

- [ ] Riley's attitude.
- [ ] Riley's uniform.
- [x] Riley's shoes.

e. Riley's school says she must wear different shoes.

- [x] Right.
- [ ] Wrong.

f. Riley's mother says the shoes are...

- [x] black leather lace-up shoes.
- [ ] pink leather lace-up shoes.
- [ ] blue leather lace-up shoes.

Third viewing

g. How does Riley feel?

- [x] Upset and angry.
- [ ] Happy and excited.

h. She does not feel happy because she can't go to school at the moment.

- [x] Right.
- [ ] Wrong.

i. Does she miss school?

- [x] Yes, she does, she wants to go back to school.
- [ ] No, she doesn't, she wants to stay at home.

CONSEILS

- Pour t'aider à comprendre la vidéo, observe bien les objets que la caméra filme et sois attentif/attentive à l'attitude et au ton des personnes.
- Il n'est pas nécessaire de tout comprendre dans la vidéo, concentre-toi sur les mots que tu connais.
- Lis attentivement les questions et les réponses proposées avant d'y répondre.

Vocabulary

- **ru**nners
- stay
- miss

B

First viewing

a. What can you say about this document? It is a video.

b. Riley is... ☑ a schoolgirl at a local school. ☐ a student at a local university.

c. What is the video about: school, uniforms, food or shoes?

The video is about school and shoes.

Second viewing

d. What is the problem? The problem is Riley's shoes.

e. Must Riley change and wear different shoes at school?

Yes, she must change and wear different shoes.

f. Riley's mother says the shoes are...
☑ black leather lace-up shoes. ☐ pink leather lace-up shoes. ☐ blue leather lace-up shoes.

Third viewing

g. How does Riley feel? She feels upset and angry.

h. Why? Because she can't go to school at the moment.

i. Does she miss school? Yes, she misses school, she wants to go back.

PREPARE YOUR FINAL TASKS

→ Book p. 23

How do you feel about Riley's problem?
Do you think uniforms at school are a good thing?
Discuss the problem with your friends.

Riley's problem is... / She wears...

Uniforms at schools are...

CONSEILS

Aide-toi du vocabulaire de la leçon précédente et utilise les adverbes de fréquence : *never*, *always*, *sometimes* et *often*.

Language practice GRAMMAR

Exprimer ses sentiments → Book p. 25

Pour exprimer mes sentiments j'utilise ...feel... + adjectif.

I ...feel happy... because this is the last day of school!

1 Complète les phrases suivantes avec l'adjectif qui convient.

nervous / happy / sick / lonely / scared

a. Oh my God, I feel ...sick... . I think I am going to vomit!

b. When I see spiders, I feel ...scared... .

c. On my first day at school I always feel ...nervous... .

d. When I meet my friends, I feel ...happy... .

e. I have no friends, I feel so ...lonely... .

There is... / There are... → Book p. 25

Pour parler de la présence de quelque chose ou de quelqu'un on utilise ...There is... + nom dénombrable au singulier / nom indénombrable ou ...There are... + nom dénombrable au pluriel.

...There is... a football ground in my school.

...There are... four computer rooms in my school.

2 Remets les mots dans l'ordre pour faire des phrases.

a. in / there / a / my / school / cinema / is / ideal.

In my ideal school, there is a cinema.

b. there / a / in / school / is / cafeteria / your / ?

Is there a cafeteria in your school?

c. are / tennis / there / courts / in / school / the / ?

Are there tennis courts in the school?

d. there / a / library / is / but / is / no / cinema / there.

There is a library but there is no cinema.

Le modal *can*

→ Book p. 25

Pour dire ce que je peux ou ne peux pas faire, j'utilise ....can..........

ou ....can't (cannot) + BV.......... .

3 Dis ce que les élèves peuvent faire ou ne pas faire dans ton école. Utilise les éléments donnés et le modal *can*.

a. Pupils / go to the library. Pupils can go to the library.

b. They / play volleyball in the playground. They can't play volleyball in the playground.

c. They / play handball in the sport court. They can play handball in the sport court.

d. They / eat lunch at the canteen. They can eat lunch at the canteen.

e. They / run in the corridors. They can't run in the corridors.

4 Lis les phrases suivantes. Corrige celles que tes professeurs ne te diront jamais.

a. At school, you can jump on the tables! At school, you can't jump on the tables!

b. You can't fight with other pupils. ....

c. You can't do your homework! You can do your homework!

d. You can dance in class. You can't dance in class.

Le présent simple

→ Book p. 25

Pour parler de mes goûts, de mes habitudes ou de généralités, j'utilise le ....présent simple.......... .

À la forme négative, j'utilise ....do + not.......... .

I ....don't (do + not).......... really like Maths.

5 Mets le verbe à la forme qui convient.

a. I (go) ....go.......... to school every day, but I (not go) ....don't go.......... to school on weekends!

b. French pupils (start) ....start.......... primary school at 6 years old.

c. After school, British pupils (go) ....go.......... to clubs or they (go) ....go.......... home but they (no / work) ....don't work.......... at school!

d. I (like) ....like.......... studying but I (not / like) ....don't like.......... sports!

e. At 11 years old, British pupils (enter) ....enter.......... "Year 6" but they (not / enter) ....don't enter.......... "6e".

6 **Réponds aux questions suivantes.**

a. Do you like school? Yes, I do. / Yes, I like school.

No, I don't. / No, I don't like school.

b. What time do you start school on Mondays? I start school at ... am.

c. What time do you finish school on Fridays? I finish school at ... pm.

d. Do you go to school on weekends? No, I don't go to school on weekends.

e. What time do British pupils finish school?

They finish school at 3.00 pm.

Le présent simple à la 3e personne du singulier et les adverbes de fréquence → Book p. 25

• À la 3e personne du singulier, il faut un -s à la fin du verbe à la forme affirmative.

Riley (go) goes to McClelland School in Frankston, Australia.

• À la forme négative do + not devient does + not.

She doesn't live in France.

• Si j'utilise un adverbe de fréquence, je le place avant le verbe.

She never takes the train to school.

7 **Mets le verbe à la forme qui convient.**

a. Riley (live) lives in Frankston, Australia so she (go) goes to school there.

b. She (wear) wears a uniform to go to school!

c. She (like) likes Art but she (not / like) does not like Maths.

d. She (take) takes the bus to school every day but she (not / ride) doesn't ride a bike to school.

8 **Fais des phrases à partir des éléments donnés en utilisant les adverbes de fréquence suivants : *always*, *never*, *sometimes* et *often*.**
N'oublie pas le « s » à la fin du verbe à la 3e personne du singulier.

a. French students / wear runners at school.

French students often wear runners at school.

b. Australian students / wear runners at school.

Australian students never wear runners at school.

c. Riley / wear a uniform at school.

Riley always wears a uniform at school.

d. She / wear a blazer.

She sometimes wears a blazer.

Le modal *must* → Book p. 26

• Pour exprimer une obligation, j'utilise must + BV.

• Pour exprimer une interdiction, j'utilise must not / mustn't + BV.

Pupils must do their homework!

They mustn't eat chewing-gum in class.

9 Remets les mots dans l'ordre.

a. pupils / an / schools / unbuttoned / wear / collar / mustn't / British / In.

In British schools, pupils mustn't wear an unbuttoned collar.

b. They / a / blazer / mustn't / rolled up / with / sleeves / wear.

They mustn't wear a blazer with rolled up sleeves.

c. Girls / make-up / and / mustn't / wear / jewellery.

Girls mustn't wear make-up and jewellery.

d. Must / have / black / trousers / formal / they / ?

Must they have black formal trousers?

e. Jumpers / be / purple / must / and / socks / be / black / must / white / or

Jumpers must be purple and socks must be black or white.

10 Réponds aux questions suivantes.

a. What colour must blazers be at Sharples School? Blazers must be graphite grey.

b. What sort of tie must they wear? They must wear a striped tie.

c. What must the pupils have on their blazer? They must have the school badge.

d. Why must they have a schoolbag? They must have a schoolbag for books and equipment.

e. What length must the skirt be? The skirt must be below the knee.

Language practice PHONOLOGY

La prononciation de *can* [kæn]et *can't* [kɑːnt] → Book p. 26

......Can...... [kæn] se prononce de façon brève.

......Can't...... [kɑːnt] se prononce de façon plus relâchée, le son dure plus longtemps.

She ......can...... speak 5 languages.

They ......can't...... play baseball in the playground.

1 ***Can* ou *can't* ? Écoute les phrases et écris leur numéro dans la colonne correspondante.** 16 CD1 16 MP3

can [kæn]	can't [kɑːnt]
1 et 4	2 et 3
5	6

La prononciation de [uː]et [aʊ] → Book p. 26

Le son [uː] est un son ......long et relâché...... .

She has got new **shoes**!

Le son [aʊ] est une diphtongue, c'est-à-dire qu'il faut entendre deux sons !

What is it **about**?

2 **Écoute les mots suivants et classe-les dans le tableau.** 18 CD1 18 MP3

room / boots / allow / cool / about / shoes / how / playground

[uː]	[aʊ]
room	allow
boots	about
cool	how
shoes	playground

Auto-évaluation

→ Book p. 30

Connaissances et compétences linguistiques

Vocabulary

- Je connais le vocabulaire relatif à l'école (activités, matières, lieux).
- Je connais le vocabulaire relatif à l'uniforme.

Grammar

- Je sais exprimer mes sentiments.
- Je sais utiliser *can* et *can't*, *must* et *mustn't*.
- Je sais parler de généralités, de goûts, d'habitude avec le présent simple et les adverbes de fréquence.

Phonology

- Je sais faire la différence entre *can* et *can't*.
- Je sais prononcer le [uː] et le [aʊ].

Compétences langagières et domaines du socle commun

Écouter et comprendre
Domaines 1, 2
- Je sais comprendre une vidéo.

Lire et comprendre
Domaines 1, 2
- Je sais repérer les informations essentielles d'un document extrait d'un site Internet.

Parler en continu
Domaines 1, 2, 3
- Je sais parler du système scolaire britannique ou américain.
- Je sais raconter ce qui se passe dans une vidéo.

Écrire
Domaines 1, 2
- Je sais rédiger un texte sur les systèmes scolaires.
- Je sais expliquer ce qu'il est possible ou non de faire dans une école.

Réagir et dialoguer
Domaines 1, 2, 3
- Je sais exprimer mes goûts et sentiments, en imaginant mon école idéale ou en comparant les systèmes scolaires.

PEAC

Culture et Parcours
Domaines 1, 2, 3, 5
- Je connais les différents aspects du système scolaire britannique ou américain.

2 Let's get cooking!

1 MasterChef Junior

GET READY! → Book p. 32

1. Who are these children?
- [x] TV contestants.
- [ ] TV presenters.

2. How do they look?
- [x] Anxious.
- [x] Nervous.
- [ ] Sad.
- [ ] Angry.

3. Where are they?
- [ ] At the school cafeteria.
- [ ] In their kitchen at home.
- [x] In a TV studio.

CONSEILS
Tu vas regarder la vidéo trois fois. Concentre-toi sur les images. Note les mots que tu ne comprends pas.

GO! VIDEO 3 → Book p. 32

Comment on the video. Choose between the following exercises (A or B).

AP ACCOMPAGNEMENT PERSONNALISÉ
DIFFÉRENCIATION

A

First viewing

a. Name the TV show.
- [ ] The Great British Bake Off
- [ ] MasterChef
- [x] MasterChef Junior

b. Who are the three adults?
- [ ] 3 famous TV presenters.
- [x] 3 famous culinary chefs.
- [ ] 3 famous contestants.

c. The children are ready to...
- [x] cook.
- [ ] taste famous chefs' dinners.

Second viewing

d. This generation of candidates is...
- [ ] old.
- [x] new and young.

e. So "Age is just...
- [x] a number"
- [ ] a joke"
- [ ] a game"

f. The children are from...
- [x] The United States of America.
- [ ] The United Kingdom.
- [ ] South America.

Third viewing

g. Which challenge are the children doing?
- [ ] A fashion challenge.
- [x] A cooking challenge.

h. Tick the compliments given to the children.
- [x] "This is about as good as it gets".
- [x] "That is perfection".
- [ ] "Congratulations".

i. In the end, the prize is...
- [ ] 1000 $
- [ ] 10000 $
- [x] 100 000 $

CONSEILS

- Lorsque tu regardes la vidéo tente d'identifier les mots que tu connais déjà. Avant de
- répondre, relis bien toutes les questions.
- Repère les termes de cuisine, cela t'aidera.

Vocabulary

- taste

B

First viewing

a. Name the TV show.

This TV show is called "MasterChef Junior".

b. Who are the three adults?

They are three famous culinary chefs.

c. The children are ready to: cook.

Second viewing

d. This generation of candidates is new and young.

e. So "Age is just... a number".

f. The children are from the United States of America.

Third viewing

g. Which challenge are the children doing?

They are doing a cooking challenge.

h. Write the compliments given to the children:

– "that is perfection"

– "this is about as good as it gets"

– "it's a technique we haven't seen in regular MasterChef"

i. In the end, what is the prize for the winner?

The prize is 100 000 $.

j. What title does the winner get?

The winner gets the title of "MasterChef Junior".

2 Breakfasts from around the world

GET READY! → Book p. 33

Look at the document and answer the questions.

1. Name the different kinds of food on the picture.

Fried eggs / sausages / mushrooms / fried tomatoes / bacon / baked beans.

2. Who do you recognize behind the food?

I can see The Beatles.

3. What is a full English breakfast?

There is some bacon. There are some fried tomatoes. There are some mushrooms and fried eggs. There are some sausages. There is some bread.

4. Why is it a funny picture?

Because...

☐ it looks like breakfast.

☑ you can see people in the food.

GO! VIDEO 4 → Book p. 33

Comment on the video. Choose between the following exercises (A or B).

ACCOMPAGNEMENT AP PERSONNALISÉ

DIFFÉRENCIATION

CONSEILS

Tu vas regarder la vidéo trois fois.
Concentre-toi sur les mots que tu as déjà vu.
Relis le vocabulaire de la page précédente.

A

First viewing

a. What document is it?

☐ A trailer for a new film. ☑ A documentary on breakfasts. ☐ A TV cooking programme.

b. Give the title of the document:

American kids try breakfasts from around the world.

c. What are the children doing in the video?

☑ They are tasting different breakfasts.

☐ They are cooking different breakfasts.

d. What is the first young boy's reaction? ☐ He looks surprised. ☐ He looks interested. ☑ He looks disgusted.

e. Where is this breakfast from? Korea

f. What is this breakfast composed of? Circle the right answers.

(soup) – (fish) – cereals – bread – (a fried egg) – vegetables – (rice) – (pickled cabbage) – coffee – tea – orange juice.

g. Look at the other children's reactions. Right or wrong?

– They look surprised, but they taste it. Right – They taste it and hate it. Right

Second viewing

h. What about the second breakfast? Where is it from? It's from Brazil

i. What can you see on the plate?

- [x] cheese
- [x] ham
- [ ] pancakes
- [x] banana
- [ ] eggs
- [ ] tea
- [x] bread
- [x] orange
- [x] coffee

Third viewing

j. They don't really like drinking coffee. (Right) / Wrong

k. The boy thinks it is ... that kids drink coffee in Brazil. [ ] funny [x] weird [ ] interesting

l. The third breakfast is from Finland

m. There is a piece of bread with fish and some fruit

n. Who likes the breakfast from Finland?

- [x] The boy with long curly dark hair.
- [ ] The girl with blond hair.
- [ ] The young Chinese boy.

B

CONSEILS

Lis attentivement chaque question avant d'y répondre. Tu vas compléter la grille en utilisant le vocabulaire vu dans la leçon et dans la vidéo. Sois attentif !

First viewing

a. What document is it?

It is a video about breakfasts from around the world.

b. Give the title of the document.

American kids try breakfasts from around the world.

c. What are the children doing in the video?

They are tasting different breakfasts.

d. What is the first young boy's reaction? He looks disgusted.

e. Where is this breakfast from?

The breakfast is from Korea.

f. What is this breakfast composed of? Write all the words you can.

soup – fish – a fried egg – rice – pickled cabbage.

g. Look at the other children's reactions. Make sentences using the following words:
like / love / hate / refuse / taste / disgusted / surprised / try / breakfast.

They are disgusted, they refuse to taste this breakfast. They try it and they hate it.

They are surprised, but they taste it.

Second viewing

h. Where is the second breakfast from? It's from Brazil.

i. What can you see on the plate? Name the different kinds of food.

Cheese – ham –a banana – bread – orange – coffee.

j. En utilisant les aliments que tu as trouvés, rédige une phrase pour décrire ce petit déjeuner.

Third viewing

k. What is their reaction after drinking coffee? They don't like it, except one boy.

l. The third breakfast is from Finland

m. There is a piece of bread with fish and some fruit.

n. Can you name the fruit? ☐ strawberries ☑ blueberries ☐ blackberries

o. Who likes the breakfast from Finland? The boy with long curly dark hair likes it.

CONSEILS

Pour dire quel est le petit déjeuner que tu as préféré, tu peux regarder la vidéo encore une fois et faire la liste des aliments que tu aimes. Puis note les expressions dont tu as besoin pour exprimer ce que tu aimes ou ce que tu n'aimes pas.

Vocabulary

- dis**gust**ed
- **pickl**ed **ca**bbage
- weird
- taste

PREPARE YOUR FINAL TASKS → Book p. 33

Describe your favourite breakfast in the video.

I like the breakfast from ... because there is some .../there are some .../There is a ... and some ...
I prefer ..., it looks ... and ...
I don't like ... because there isn't any ... There aren't any ...

3 Love our food

GET READY!

→ Book p. 34

Look at the document and answer the questions below.

1. Who is this man?

a. What's his name?

His name is Jamie Oliver.

b. What's his nationality?

He is...

☐ American. ☑ British. ☐ Australian.

2. What's his job?

a. What does he do?

- ☑ He is a chef.
- ☑ He is a TV presenter.
- ☑ He is a restaurateur.
- ☐ He writes novels.
- ☐ He is a comedian.
- ☑ He writes cookery books.

b. What is his speciality?

Italian cuisine.

c. What does he use when cooking?

He uses local produce and quality ingredients.

3. Why is he famous?

a. He is famous because...

- ☐ he is very rich.
- ☑ he presents several shows on TV.
- ☑ he fights against bad eating habits.

b. What are the unhealthy foods? Tick the correct answers.

☑ sweets	☐ milk	☑ crisps	☐ fruit	☑ hamburger	☑ soda
☑ cookies	☐ fish	☑ hot-dog	☑ chips	☐ water	☐ vegetables

GO! VIDEO → Book p. 34

Comment on the video. Choose between the following exercises (A or B).

AP ACCOMPAGNEMENT PERSONNALISÉ — DIFFÉRENCIATION

CONSEILS
Regarde la vidéo trois fois. Concentre-toi sur les mots que tu connais déjà. Aide-toi des images pour comprendre.

A

First viewing

a. This video is...
- ☐ a cartoon.
- ☐ a documentary.
- ☑ a filmed recipe for a TV show.

b. Who are the two blond little girls?
- ☐ Milly and Penny.
- ☑ Daisy and Poppy.
- ☐ Lili and Jenny.

Second viewing

c. What recipe is Jamie Oliver doing in the video? He is making...
- ☑ American pancakes.
- ☐ a cake.
- ☐ a fruit salad.

d. What are the ingredients? Tick the correct words.
- ☑ Milk.
- ☐ Chocolate.
- ☑ Flour.
- ☐ Sugar.
- ☑ Salt.
- ☑ Egg.
- ☐ Apple.

Third viewing

e. Describe the recipe step by step. Put a number on the actions needed to bake a cake.

– Pour the flour in the bowl! ....(1)....

– Add an egg! ....(3)....

– Whisk everything! ....(5)....

– Pour the milk into the bowl! ....(2)....

– Put a little pinch of salt in the bowl! ....(4)....

– Grate some fruit in it then stir again! ....(6)....

– Make little piles in the pan and cook the pancakes! ....(7)....

B

First viewing

a. What sort of video is it? It is...
- ☐ an extract from a film.
- ☐ a report.
- ☑ a filmed recipe for a TV show.

b. Who are the two little girls with Jamie Oliver?
- ☐ Milly and Penny.
- ☑ Daisy and Poppy.
- ☐ Lili and Jenny.

c. They are...
- ☐ two little chefs.
- ☐ 6 years old.
- ☑ Jamie Oliver's daughters.

Second viewing

d. What recipe is Jamie Oliver doing in the video?

He is making ...American pancakes....

e. What are the ingredients? Complete the list with the name of the ingredients.

– a teacup of ...self-raising flour...

– a teacup of ...milk...

– a little pinch of ...salt...

– one ...egg...

– some grated ...pear... or ...raspberry... or ...banana... or ...blueberry...

or ...blackberry... or ...strawberry...!

Third viewing

e. Describe the recipe step by step. Put a number on the actions needed to bake a cake.

– Pour the flour in the bowl! ...(2)...

– Pour some flour in a teacup! ...(1)...

– Add an egg! ...(5)...

– Measure the milk with the teacup! ...(3)...

– Whisk everything and do little movements first! ...(7)...

– Pour the milk into the bowl! ...(4)...

– Put a little pinch of salt in the bowl! ...(6)...

– Heat some butter in a pan! ...(10)...

– Make big movements when it gets mixed up! ...(8)...

– Grate some fruit in it then stir again! ...(9)...

– Make little piles in the pan and cook the pancakes! ...(11)...

Vocabulary

- a **tea**cup
- self-**rai**sing flour
- a pinch
- **gra**ted
- **rasp**berry
- **blue**berry
- **black**berry
- a pan

- pour
- add
- whisk
- heat
- stir

4 School lunches

GET READY! → Book p. 35

Look at the documents and answer the questions.

1. What do you see?

I see two pictures with food, maybe they are lunches.

2. What food do you identify?

a. Connect each word to the corresponding image.

nuggets / ketchup / a cookie / fruit / peas / mashed potatoes / melon / baked beans / sausages / sweetcorn / baked potato

b. Write a sentence mentioning the food you recognize.

I recognize nuggets, ketchup, a cookie, fruit, peas, mashed potatoes, sausages, baked beans, sweetcorn...

sausages — a cookie — fruit

baked beans — sweetcorn — peas

melon — baked potato — mashed potatoes — nuggets — ketchup

3. What countries are these lunches from?

a. They are from the UK and the USA.

b. Complete the sentence: They look very...

- [x] similar.
- [ ] different.
- [ ] strange-looking.
- [ ] tasty.
- [x] unhealthy.

GO! → Book p. 35

Read and comment on the text.

www.nytimes.com

Why students hate school lunches?

MORE than 30 million children trundle[1] through school cafeteria lines every day in the United States and thanks to the Healthy, Hunger-Free Kids Act, which took[2] effect in 2012, they are no longer served[3] greasy[4] pizza, salty[5] French fries and sauced up[6] chicken wings. Meals must now be lower in fat[7], calories and sodium and contain lean[8] proteins, more fruits and vegetables and whole grains.

1. avancer lentement, se traîner – 2. a pris effet – 3. servi – 4. gras – 5. salé – 6. accompagné de sauce – 7. plus faible en gras – 8. maigre

CONSEILS

Lis attentivement le texte. Tu y trouveras toutes les réponses aux questions. Note les mots que tu ne comprends pas.

ACCOMPAGNEMENT PERSONNALISÉ AP

DIFFÉRENCIATION

Choose between the following exercises (A or B).

A

First reading

a. What is the text about? Identify the document. It is...
- [ ] a letter.
- [x] an article from a website.
- [ ] an extract from a book.

b. Identify the topic of the document. It is a document about...
- [ ] music.
- [x] food.
- [x] school meals in the USA.
- [ ] restaurants.

c. Tick the food that is unhealthy.
- [ ] Fruit.
- [x] Salty French fries.
- [x] Greasy pizza.
- [ ] Vegetables.
- [ ] Whole grains.
- [x] Chicken wings.

Second reading

d. Say what you understand. "30 million" is...
- [ ] the population of the USA.
- [x] the number of children eating in school cafeterias.

e. What happened in 2012?
- [ ] The government authorized nuggets, French fries and other unhealthy food in school cafeterias.
- [x] The government banned unhealthy food in schools cafeterias.
- [x] The government decided school cafeterias must serve healthy food.

f. Write the date you see:

2012

Third reading

g. What sort of meals must American children eat now? They must...
- [x] eat fruit and vegetables in schools.
- [ ] eat fries and nuggets.
- [ ] eat salty and greasy food.
- [ ] hamburgers and pizza.
- [x] eat whole grain foods.
- [ ] eat too many calories.

h. Say what "healthy" means.
- [x] Good for you.
- [ ] Bad for you.
- [x] Lower in fat and sodium.

B

First reading

a. Identify the document. It is an article from a website.

b. What is the text about?

It is an article about food served in American schools.

c. Make a list of the food which is...

– good for your health:

fruit / vegetables / whole grains food / lean proteins.

– bad for your health:

French fries / nuggets / chicken wings / hamburgers / pizzas / sodas.

Second reading

d. Say what you understand. How many children eat at school cafeterias in the USA?

More than 30 million.

e. What happened in 2012?

- [ ] The government authorized nuggets, French fries and other unhealthy food in school cafeterias.
- [x] The government banned unhealthy food in school cafeterias.
- [x] The government decided school cafeterias must serve healthy food.

f. It refers to...

- [ ] an important decision.
- [ ] a historical event.
- [x] a government act.

g. Find the name of this act. Healthy, Hunger-Free Act

Third reading

h. What sort of meals must American children eat now?

They must only eat healthy food, they must eat food lower in fat and sodium, they must not eat too many calories. They must not eat greasy pizza and other unhealthy food.

CONSEILS

Relis le texte et toutes les questions. À la maison, relis les mots que tu ne connais pas et mémorise les mots-clefs de la leçon.

Vocabulary

- a **gov**ernment act
- an ev**ent**
- ban

CONSEILS

Pour parler d'un repas typique dans une école française, fais l'inventaire des menus que tu as mangés et une liste des plats servis. Explique si tu as le choix entre plusieurs plats.

PREPARE YOUR FINAL TASKS → Book p. 35

Talk about French school lunches.

In France, school lunches are..., with... and a lot of..., Students can choose between...

5 Lunchboxes

GET READY!

→ Book p. 36

Look at the document and answer the questions.

1. Who can you see on the photo?

I can see a little / young / blond girl.

2. What has she got on her school desk?

a. She has got... ☐ a video-game. ☑ a lunchbox. ☐ a cat.

b. What time do you think it is?

It is... ☐ midnight ☑ midday ☐ 6 pm

3. What is the young girl doing?

a. She is... ☐ doing her homework.
☐ reading a book.
☑ having lunch.

b. Where do you think she is?

She is... ☑ at school. ☐ at home. ☐ at the beach.

GO!

→ Book p. 36

Read the text and do the following exercises.

CONSEILS

- Lis la recette plusieurs fois et souligne les mots que tu connais déjà. Entoure ensuite ceux qui te sont inconnus.
- Regarde la structure de la recette pour t'aider à en comprendre les différentes étapes.

Tasty chicken wraps

Ingredients:
- 4 soft flour[1] tortillas
- 4 tbsp lower fat soft cheese[2]
- 4 tbsp low-fat natural yoghurt
- 120g boneless[3] roast chicken breasts[4] chopped[5]
- 100g sweetcorn
- ¼ cucumber
- 1 pinch[6] black pepper
- 2 handfuls[7] lettuce leaves

Serves: 4 adults

Preparation time: 15 mins

What to do:
1. Lay out the tortillas on a clean work surface.
2. Put the soft cheese and yoghurt in a bowl and mix together until smooth.
3. Add the chicken, sweetcorn and cucumber. Add some pepper, mix well. Spread some mix over each tortilla and top with lettuce.
4. Roll up each wrap, slice in half, then wrap it in cellophane and keep in the fridge before serving.

www.change4lifewales.org.uk

1. farine – 2. fromage à pâte molle – 3. sans os – 4. blancs de poulet – 5. hâchés – 6. une pincée – 7. poignées

5 Lunchboxes

ACCOMPAGNEMENT PERSONNALISÉ AP

DIFFÉRENCIATION

Comment on the text. Choose between the following exercises (A or B).

A

First reading

a. What recipe is it? It is a...

- ☐ chicken salad recipe.
- ☐ chicken couscous recipe.
- ☑ chicken wraps recipe.

b. What ingredients do you need? Tick the correct ingredients.

- ☑ chicken
- ☑ salad
- ☐ fish
- ☑ yoghurt
- ☑ tortilla
- ☐ tomato
- ☑ soft cheese
- ☑ sweetcorn
- ☑ cucumber
- ☑ pepper

Second reading

c. How much of these ingredients do you need? Tick the correct answers.

Chicken:
- ☐ 100g
- ☑ 120g

Salad:
- ☑ 2 handfuls
- ☐ 3 handfuls

Yoghurt:
- ☑ 4 tbsp
- ☐ 1 tbsp

Tortilla:
- ☐ 5
- ☑ 4

Soft cheese:
- ☐ 2 tbsp
- ☑ 4 tbsp

Sweetcorn:
- ☑ 100g
- ☐ 300g

Cucumber:
- ☑ 1/4
- ☐ 2

Pepper:
- ☑ 1 pinch
- ☐ 4 pinch

Third reading

d. What other information can you find? How many people does this recipe serve?

- ☐ 3
- ☐ 6
- ☑ 4

e. How long does it take to prepare it?

- ☐ 1 hour.
- ☑ 15 minutes.
- ☐ 50 minutes.

B

First reading

a. What recipe is it? It is a chicken wraps recipe.

b. You can eat them as... ☐ a snack. ☑ a packed lunch. ☐ dinner.

Second reading

c. What ingredients do you need and what quantities? Write names and quantities.

Meat: Chicken breasts / 120g

Vegetables: Salad / 2 handfuls; Cucumber / 4 tbsp; Corn / 100g

Dairy: Yoghurt / 4 tbsp; Soft cheese / 4 tbsp

Condiment: Pepper / 1 pinch

Starchy food: Tortillas / 4

Third reading

d. What other information can you find on this recipe? How many people does this recipe serve? It serves 4 adults.

e. How long does it take to prepare it? It takes 15 mins to prepare it.

CONSEILS

Relis la recette attentivement et fais une liste des ingrédients. Repère les quantités demandées et associe-les aux ingrédients. Essaie de déterminer à quelle catégorie d'aliments chaque ingrédient appartient avant de répondre aux questions

Vocabulary

- tablespoon (tbsp)
- **dai**ry
- a **pi**nch
- **star**chy food: *féculent*

6 Nadiya's recipe

GET READY!

→ Book p. 37

Look at the document and answer the questions.

1. Who is the lady with the hat?

She is... ☑ the Queen. ☐ a duchess.

2. Who is the cake for?

a. It is for... ☑ the Queen. ☐ British citizens.

b. What is the occasion?

☑ The Queen's birthday. ☐ An official ceremony.

3. Why is Nadiya famous?

She is famous because she has...

☑ won the Great British Bake off's contest. ☐ won a Nobel Prize.

GO!

VIDEO

→ Book p. 37

Comment on the video. Choose between the following exercises (A or B).

ACCOMPAGNEMENT PERSONNALISÉ AP

DIFFÉRENCIATION

CONSEILS

- Regarde la vidéo trois fois. Concentre-toi sur les mots que tu connais déjà.

A

First viewing

a. Nadiya is...

☐ a restaurant worker.
☐ a MasterChef TV presenter.
☑ a famous English cook.

b. Nadiya is the person chosen to...

☐ make a chocolate cake.
☑ make a birthday cake.
☐ make cupcakes.

c. It is for...

☐ Prince William's 40th birthday.
☑ Queen Elizabeth II's 90th birthday.
☐ Prince George and Princess Charlotte's next Christmas.

Second viewing

d. Give details about her task. Some of the ingredients are...

☐ lemons.
☑ marmalade.
☐ strawberry jam.
☐ maple syrup.
☐ apricots.
☐ yoghurt.
☑ oranges.
☑ buttercream.

e. Describe Nadiya's feelings. What does she think?

☐ Nadiya thinks the Queen loves oranges.
☐ Nadiya thinks the Queen hates oranges.
☑ Nadiya does not know if the Queen likes oranges.

Third viewing

f. What is Nadiya's first reaction?

☐ She is very happy.
☑ She thinks it is a prank.
☐ She is sad.

g. Her husband and daughter think...

☑ Nadiya can do it.
☐ Nadiya can't do it.

h. How does she feel about giving the cake to the Queen?

☑ Excited.
☑ Impatient.
☐ Calm.
☐ Indifferent.
☑ Nervous.
☑ Honoured.

6 Nadiya's recipe

B

First viewing

a. What does Nadiya do for a living?

She is a famous English cook.

b. What is Nadiya's task?

She is chosen to make a birthday cake.

c. Whose birthday is it?

It is Queen Elizabeth II's 90th birthday.

Second viewing

d. Give detail about her task. List the ingredients Nadiya needs to make her cake.

To make her cake, she needs marmalade, oranges, buttercream...

e. Does Nadiya know if the Queen likes oranges?

No, she does not know if the Queen likes oranges.

Third viewing

f. Describe Nadiya's feelings.

At first, she thinks it is a mistake or a prank.

g. What do her husband and daughter think about this challenge?

They think Nadiya can do it.

h. How does she feel about giving the cake to the Queen?

She feels excited, impatient, nervous and honoured.

CONSEILS

Sois attentif et regarde bien ce que fait Nadiya. Note les mots que tu ne connais pas et essaie de repérer les mots-clefs.

Vocabulary

- a prank
- choose/chosen
- need
- feel

PREPARE YOUR FINAL TASKS

→ Book p. 37

You want to make a chocolate cake for your best friend's birthday. List all the ingredients and tell your mum or dad what they need to buy at the supermarket.

I need ... / Please, buy ... / Don't forget ... / Take some ...

CONSEILS

Prépare une liste d'ingrédients pour la recette. Révise les verbes dont tu as besoin pour donner des instructions et pense à utiliser l'impératif.

Some / Any

→ Book p. 39

Pour exprimer la quantité, j'utilise :
• dans les phrases affirmatives : ......some...... + nom indénombrable / dénombrable pluriel.

Ex. : There is ......some...... ham. There are ......some...... oranges.

• dans les phrases négatives : **not** ......any...... ou **no**.

Ex. : There is **not** ......any...... cheese / there is **no** cheese.

There are **not** ......any...... tomatoes / there are **no** tomatoes.

• dans les phrases interrogatives : ......any...... ou ......some...... (si l'on est certain d'une réponse positive).

Ex. : Is there ......any...... milk? *Ex. :* Do you want ......some...... help?

1 Complète avec *some*, *any* ou *not any*.

a. There is ......some...... bread on the table.

b. There are ......not any...... bananas in the bowl.

c. Are there ......any...... sweets in the cupboard?

d. I can see ......some...... apples on the plate.

e. Is there ......any...... orange juice in the fridge?

f. Can I taste ......some...... cake, please?

2 Utilise *some* ou *any* dans les phrases suivantes.

a. In an English breakfast, there is ......some...... ham and there are ......some...... oranges.

b. I can eat ......some...... cheese but I can't eat ......any...... yoghurt.

L'impératif

→ Book p. 39

Pour donner un ordre, une injonction, j'utilise : ......BV + !...... à la forme affirmative.

......Don't + BV + !...... à la forme négative.

3 Tu es le chef de ton restaurant. Donne des ordres à tes commis.

a. prepare / the cakes. Prepare the cakes!

b. not put / too much salt. Don't put too much salt!

c. bake / for 30 mins. Bake for 30 mins!

How much / How many → Book p. 40

Pour poser une question sur une quantité, j'utilise : how much + indénombrable

how many + dénombrable pluriel

4 Remets les mots dans l'ordre.

a. bread / how / do / much / want / you / ?

How much bread do you want?

b. bottles / many / orange juice / are / how / of / there / ?

How many bottles of orange juice are there?

c. many / biscuits / how / want / you / do / ?

How many biscuits do you want?

d. apple juice / much / do / how / you / need / ?

How much apple juice do you need?

Language practice PHONOLOGY

L'accentuation des mots se terminant par *-ion* → Book p. 40

1 Écoute les mots et souligne la syllabe accentuée.
Que remarques-tu pour les mots qui se terminent par *-ion* ? 29 CD1 29 MP3

Ex. : « solution » : « solution » car la syllabe accentuée est « lu ».

perfect perfection competition compete congratulate congratulation celebrate

celebration generate generation explain explanation

Je remarque que les mots en *-ion* sont toujours accentués sur l'avant-dernière syllabe.

L'intonation des phrases à l'impératif → Book p. 40

2 Lis ces phrases. Que fait la voix à la fin de chaque phrase ?

a. Fry the vegetables into a pan!
b. Don't use too much oil!
c. Cut the carrots into slices!
d. Pour the ingredients into the mixer!
e. Eat the cake when it's cool!
f. Bake the cake!

Auto-évaluation

Connaissances et compétences linguistiques

Vocabulary

- Je connais le vocabulaire des ingrédients et de la nourriture.
- Je connais le vocabulaire des ustensiles de cuisine.
- Je connais le vocabulaire utilisé dans une recette de cuisine.

Grammar

- Je sais utiliser l'impératif.
- Je sais utiliser *some*, *any* et les autres quantifieurs.
- Je sais poser des questions sur les quantités avec *how much* et *how many*.

Phonology

- Je connais l'accentuation des mots qui se terminent par *-ion*.
- Je connais l'intonation descendante des phrases à l'impératif.

Compétences langagières et domaines du socle commun

Écouter et comprendre
Domaines 1, 2

- Je sais comprendre l'essentiel des instructions d'une recette en vidéo.
- Je sais comprendre un interview.

Lire et comprendre
Domaines 1, 2

- Je sais comprendre une recette à l'écrit.
- Je sais lire et comprendre les points essentiels d'un article de journal.

Parler en continu
Domaines 1, 2, 3

- Je sais présenter une recette à l'oral.
- Je sais raconter ce qui se passe dans une vidéo.

Écrire
Domaines 1, 2

- Je sais rédiger une recette originale.

Réagir et dialoguer
Domaines 1, 2, 3

- Je sais exprimer mes goûts et opinions.

PEAC

Culture et Parcours
Domaines 1, 2, 3, 5

- Je connais des recettes typiquement anglo-saxonnes.
- Je connais des chefs britanniques et américains.
- Je connais les habitudes alimentaires des enfants américains.

3 New York, New York

1 New York

GET READY!

→ Book p. 46

1. **What sort of document is it?**

a. It is... ☐ a comic strip. ☐ an article in a newspaper. ☑ a map of New York.

b. Can you find New York's nickname in the document? It's The Big Apple.

2. **Name at least 5 famous buildings or places you can find on the map.**

→ the Statue of Liberty.

→ Ellis Island.

→ the Empire State Building.

→ Central Park.

→ the Chrysler Building.

3. **Name all the types of food you see. Why are they on the map?**

a. I can see a pizza, a hamburger with a soda, a hot-dog and some pop-corn.

b. They are on the map, because they are very ... in the USA. ☑ famous and popular ☐ rare ☐ expensive

GO! VIDEO 5 → Book p. 46

Comment on the video. Choose between the following exercises (A or B).

AP ACCOMPAGNEMENT PERSONNALISÉ DIFFÉRENCIATION

CONSEILS
- Regarde la vidéo trois fois.
- Repère les bâtiments et les lieux que tu as vu sur la carte p. 46.

A

First viewing

a. What sort of document is it?

It's...
- ☐ a short video about New York's famous restaurants.
- ☐ a documentary on the history of New York.
- ☑ a short video on New York's top attractions.

b. Who is it for?
- ☐ People who want to move to New York.
- ☐ People who live in New York.
- ☑ Tourists who want to visit New York.

c. How many attractions are there?

There are 10 main attractions.

Second viewing

d. Can you give the names of these attractions? Watch the video again and identify the places and the pictures. Then write their place/position in the top ten list.

- The Statue of Liberty (1).
- Rockefeller Center (5).
- Wall Street (7).
- Brooklyn Bridge (9).
- Central Park (4).
- The Empire State Building (3).
- Times Square (2).
- Grand Central Terminal (6).
- Greenwich Village (8).
- Staten Island Ferry (10).

Third viewing

Write down information about these attractions.

e. Brooklyn Bridge was built in...
- ☐ 1983.
- ☑ 1883.

f. Rockefeller Center is famous for...
- ☑ its tower.
- ☑ its Christmas tree.
- ☐ its museum.

g. In Central Park, people can...
- ☐ swim.
- ☑ practise outdoor activities.
- ☐ work.

h. The Statue of Liberty is...
- ☑ an American icon.
- ☐ a boring place to visit.
- ☑ the ultimate symbol of New York City.

B

First viewing

a. What sort of document is it?

It's a short video on New York's top attractions.

b. Who is it for? It is a video for people who want to visit New York.

c. How many attractions are there?

There are 10 main attractions.

Second viewing

d. Can you give the names of these attractions? Watch the video again and identify the places and the pictures. Then write their place/position in the top ten list.

CONSEILS
- Prends des notes au brouillon et écris les noms des monuments en abrégé pour gagner du temps !
- *Ex. : The Statue of Liberty = S of L*
- Sois attentif aux mots que tu ne connais pas !

1. The Statue of Liberty / 2. Times Square / 3. The Empire State Building /
4. Central Park / 5. Rockefeller Center / 6. Grand Central Terminal / 7. Wall Street /
8. Greenwich Village / 9. Brooklyn Bridge / 10. Staten Island Ferry

Third viewing

e. Brooklyn Bridge was built in 1883.

f. What is Rockefeller Center famous for?

It's famous for its tower and its Christmas tree.

g. Complete the sentence.

In Central Park, people can watch New Yorkers practise outdoor activities.

h. What does the Statue of Liberty represent?

It represents the ultimate symbol of the USA.

Vocabulary

- **har**bour
- suspe**n**sion **bri**dge = bridge supported by cables
- **b**illion = one thousand million
- **land**mark = well known monument
- un**ma**tched
- be in **awe** = admire
- go for a stroll = go for a walk

2 An artist in the city

GET READY! → Book p. 47

1. Circle the words describing the picture.

incredible scientist happy same
the countryside black and white
different artist ad the city bad colourful

2. Now answer the questions.

a. Describe this man.
- [x] He is a young artist.
- [ ] He is a photographer.
- [ ] He is a tourist.

b. What can you see behind him?
- [x] An immense drawing.
- [ ] A cartoon.
- [ ] A painting.

GO! VIDEO 6 → Book p. 47

Comment on the video. Choose between the following exercises (A or B).

AP ACCOMPAGNEMENT PERSONNALISÉ — DIFFÉRENCIATION

CONSEILS
Avant de répondre aux questions, prends le temps de regarder plusieurs fois la vidéo. Prends des notes sur ce que dit Stephen et commence à réfléchir aux lieux que tu aimes dans ta ville.

A

First viewing

a. What is Stephen's talent?
- [x] He can draw.
- [ ] He can paint.
- [ ] He can dance ballet.

b. His creations are...
- [ ] beautiful portraits.
- [x] beautiful panoramas.

c. He can do that thanks to...
- [ ] photos.
- [ ] magazines.
- [x] his visual memory.

Second viewing

d. Where is it?
- [x] In New York City.
- [ ] In San Francisco.
- [ ] In Washington D.C.

e. His creation today is...
- [ ] a forty-foot cityscape.
- [ ] a thirty-foot cityscape.
- [x] a twenty-foot cityscape.

f. Name 5 important places from the video:
- [x] Brooklyn.
- [ ] Harlem.
- [ ] The Bronx.
- [x] The George Washington Bridge.
- [ ] Chinatown.
- [x] Manhattan.
- [x] New Jersey.
- [ ] Times Square.
- [x] The Financial District.
- [x] Liberty Island.

Third viewing

g. To make this beautiful cityscape, Stephen took...
- [ ] a plane.
- [x] a helicopter.
- [ ] a boat.

h. It was...
- [ ] a twelve-minute helicopter ride.
- [x] a twenty-minute helicopter ride.

i. What is Stephen's favourite part of the city?
- [ ] Chinatown.
- [ ] Midtown.
- [x] Manhattan.

j. Why ? Choose the things he likes.
- [x] Skyscrapers.
- [x] Avenues.
- [ ] Cars.
- [x] Cabs.
- [ ] People.
- [ ] Museums.

B

First viewing

a. What is Stephen's talent? He can draw.

b. What are his creations? His creations are beautiful panoramas.

c. He can do that thanks to his visual memory.

Second viewing

d. Where is it? It is in New York City.

e. His creation today is... [ ] a forty-foot cityscape. [ ] a thirty-foot cityscape. [x] a twenty-foot cityscape.

f. Name 5 important places from the video:

Brooklyn, the George Washington Bridge, Manhattan, New Jersey, the Financial District and Liberty Island.

Third viewing

g. To make this beautiful cityscape, Stephen took a helicopter.

h. It was... ☐ a twelve-minute helicopter ride. ☑ a twenty-minute helicopter ride.

i. What is Stephen's favourite part of the city? His favourite part of the city is Manhattan.

j. Why?

Because he likes skyscrapers, avenues and cabs.

PREPARE YOUR FINAL TASKS → Book p. 47

Just like Stephen Wiltshire, speak about your favourite place in your city.

In my city there is a place I really like, it is called ... / My favourite place in my city is ... because ...

Vocabulary

- thanks to
- take / took

3 Coney Island

GET READY! → Book p. 48

1. Look at the picture. Match the words to the corresponding number.

a ferris wheel / a carnival ride / a theme park / the seaside / buildings / the sand

1. buildings
2. a ferris wheel
3. a theme park
4. the sand
5. the seaside
6. a carnival ride

2. What can you see? Where is it?

a. I can see... ☐ people in the mountains. ☑ people by the seaside. ☐ people going to work.

b. Where is it? It is... ☑ in Coney Island, near New York. ☐ far away from the city.

3. What are the people doing? (multiple answers)

☑ They are swimming.
☑ They are having fun.
☐ They are working.
☑ They are sunbathing.
☑ They are relaxing.
☐ They are dancing.

GO! → Book p. 48

Read and comment on the text.

CONSEILS

- Lis le texte plusieurs fois. Souligne les mots que tu connais déjà. N'aie pas peur de ne pas tout comprendre.

Hit the Beach!

Two centuries of beachgoers can't be wrong: the surf and sand[1] are the real reason to go here. Weekend after weekend, Coney Island is the most crowded[2] – especially in the area in front of Luna Park – and Brighton is second. If you want a little room, go to the stretch[3] of sand between the two. There are no shops in the immediate area so pack a picnic or be prepared to flag down[4] the vendors who sell cotton candy, ice cream, cocktails, and more. (Also: if you've got a beach umbrella, bring it. You can buy one at one of the many stores on the way to the beach, too.) Beaches are open with lifeguards[5] on duty[6] from 10 am to 5 pm.

To go to Coney Island: take the D, Q, N or F train to Stillwell Avenue.

To go to Brighton Beach: take the B or Q to Brighton Beach.

Adapted from: www.redtri.com

1. sable - 2. bondé - 3. l'étendue - 4. héler, faire signe - 5. maître nageur - 6. être de service

Choose between the following exercises (A or B).

AP Accompagnement personnalisé — DIFFÉRENCIATION

A

First reading

a. What is the article about?
☐ A place called Island Park.
☑ A place called Coney Island.
☑ A place where people from New York go to on weekends.
☐ A place where you can eat at different restaurants.

b. "beachgoers": what words do you identify? ....beach........ and ....go........ .
→ Can you guess what it means?

It means people who go to the beach.

Second reading

c. Why do people go to Coney Island?
☑ To surf and relax. ☐ To work. ☑ To swim and sunbathe. ☐ To visit museums.

d. Right or Wrong? Circle the right answers. Correct if necessary.

New Yorkers go to Coney Island to surf and relax. (R) / W

Every weekend, Coney Island is empty. R / (W)

"Coney Island is the most crowded".

You can't have a picnic in Coney Island. R / (W)

"Pack a picnic".

In Coney Island there is a beach and a theme park. (R) / W

You can eat ice cream and cotton candy. (R) / W

Third reading

e. What will you do when you are there?

- [x] You will sunbathe.
- [x] You will eat cotton candy and ice cream.
- [ ] You will go to a restaurant.
- [x] You will bring a beach umbrella.
- [ ] You will drink cocktails.
- [x] You will see lifeguards.

B

First reading

a. What is the article about? The article is about a place called Coney Island.

b. "beachgoers": what words do you identify? beach and go.

→ Can you guess what it means? It means people who go to the beach.

Second reading

c. Why do people go to Coney Island?

People go to Coney Island on weekends to have fun and relax.

d. Right or Wrong? Justify your answers by quoting the text.

– Lots of people go there. Right: "Coney Island is the most crowded"

– There are lots of shops around. Wrong: "there are no shops"

Third reading

e. Check the last two lines. What train will you take to go...

– to Coney Island: I will take the D, Q, N or F train.

– to Brighton Beach: I will take the B or Q train.

CONSEILS

Lis le texte attentivement. Repère les noms propres, les activités, les mots qui se réfèrent à la nourriture. Souligne d'une couleur différente chaque type de mots. À la maison, relis tes notes et cherche la signification des mots que tu ne connais pas.

Vocabulary

- **crow**ded = full of people
- stretch = area/space
- **flag** down = make a sign

4 Skyscrapers!

GET READY! → Book p. 49

Look at the document and answer the questions.

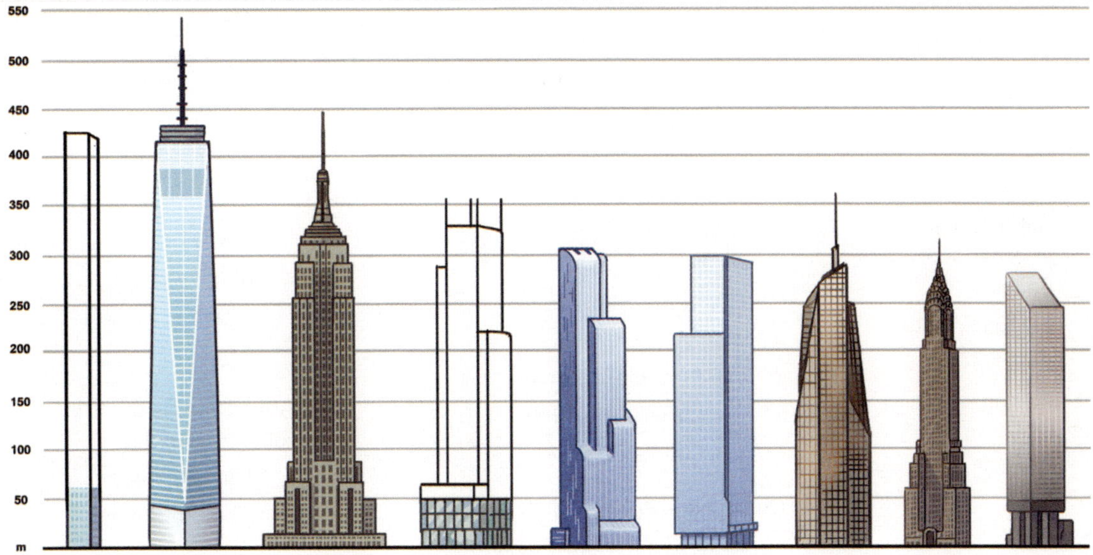

Name	432 Park Avenue	One World Trade Center	Empire State Building	Three World Trade Center	One 57	Four World Trade Center	Bank of America Tower	Chrysler Building	Citigroup Center
Year	2016	2013	1931	2014	2013	2013	2009	1930	1977
Floors	89	105	102	80	75	72	55	77	59
Height	426 m	546 m	443 m	357 m	306 m	298 m	366 m	319 m	279 m

4 Skyscrapers!

1. What can you see?

a. I can see... ☐ houses. ☐ sculptures. ☑ very high buildings called "skyscrapers".

b. Where is it? ☐ In London. ☑ In New York City. ☐ In Dublin.

2. Compare the buildings. Tick the correct sentences.

☐ The Empire State Building is higher than the One World Trade Center.

☑ The One World Trade Center is higher than the Empire State Building.

☑ The Chrysler Building is older than the Empire State Building.

☐ The Empire State Building is older than the Chrysler Building.

GO! VIDEO 7

→ Book p. 49

Comment the video. Choose between the following exercises (A or B).

AP ACCOMPAGNEMENT PERSONNALISÉ

DIFFÉRENCIATION

A

First viewing

a. What is the video about?
- ☑ A skyscraper in N.Y.C. (New York City).
- ☐ A skyscraper in L.A. (Los Angeles).

b. This skyscraper's name is...
- ☐ the Chrysler Building.
- ☐ the American International Building.
- ☑ the Empire State Building.

c. It takes an entire city block so it is extremely...
- ☑ big.
- ☐ small.

d. Its mail postcode is:
- ☐ 75000.
- ☐ 10LL18.
- ☑ 10118.

Second viewing

e. What can you see from the top?
- ☑ The Brooklyn Bridge.
- ☑ Central Park.
- ☑ The Rockefeller Plaza.
- ☑ The United Nations.
- ☑ The Yankee Stadium.
- ☐ Hyde Park.
- ☑ Broadway.
- ☑ Madison Square Garden.
- ☐ The Eiffel Tower.
- ☑ Times Square.
- ☐ Big Ben.
- ☐ The White House.
- ☑ Wall Street.
- ☑ The Statue of Liberty.
- ☑ The Chrysler Building.
- ☑ The Citi Field.

f. On a clear day, you can see...
- ☐ up to 18 miles (28,962 km).
- ☑ up to 80 miles (128,72 km).

Third viewing

g. Describe this building. After one year and 45 days, it was inaugurated in...
- ☐ 1929.
- ☐ 1930.
- ☑ 1931.

h. So, it was built in...
- ☐ 1929.
- ☑ 1930.
- ☐ 1931.

i. How many floors has it got?
- ☐ 82.
- ☑ 102.
- ☐ 92.

j. What floor is the first observation deck?
- ☐ The 68th floor.
- ☑ The 86th floor.

CONSEILS

- La vidéo porte sur un monument, concentre-toi pour tenter de comprendre le plus d'éléments possible. Repère les termes que tu as déjà vus dans les leçons précédentes

B

First viewing

a. What is the video about?

It is about a skyscraper in New York City.

b. What is this skyscraper's name?

This skyscraper's name is the Empire State Building.

c. It takes an entire city block so it is extremely... ☑ big. ☐ small.

d. What is its mail postcode? It is 10118.

Second viewing

e. What can you see from the top? Name all the buildings you can.

I can see the Brooklyn Bridge, Central Park, South Street Seaport, the Rockefeller Plaza, the United Nations, the Yankee Stadium, Broadway, the Meadowlands Sports Complex, Madison Square Garden, Times Square, the Intrepid Air and Space Museum, the Javits Convention Center, Wall Street, the Statue of Liberty, the Chrysler Building and the Citi Field.

f. On a clear day, you can see...
☐ up to 18 miles (28,962 km). ☑ up to 80 miles (128,72 km).

Third viewing

g. Describe this building. When was it inaugurated?

It was inaugurated in 1931.

h. When was it built?

It was built in 1930.

Vocabulary

- city block
- up to
- built in

CONSEILS

Tu ne vas pas pouvoir noter le nom de tous les monuments, concentre-toi sur ceux que tu connais déjà et essaie d'écrire le maximum de noms que tu peux.

CONSEILS TICE

Aide-toi du document de la page 46 de ton workbook pour pouvoir facilement comparer les monuments. Tu peux aussi aller sur Internet. Tu y trouveras de nombreuses informations sur tous les monuments de New York !

PREPARE YOUR FINAL TASKS

→ Book p. 49

Choose two skyscrapers in New York City and compare them.
X is ... meters high so it is higher than Y.
Z is ... meters high so it is lower than X.

5 High Line Park

GET READY!

→ Book p. 50

Look and react.

1. Who and what can you see?

a. I can see...

- [x] pedestrians walking.
- [ ] people running in a park.
- [ ] people sleeping in the sun.

b. I can see...

- [x] a bridge lined with plants.
- [ ] a bridge made of bricks.
- [ ] a bridge with many cars.

2. What do you think it is?

I think it is...

- [ ] a walking bridge.
- [x] a new modern park.
- [ ] a private garden.

3. Where is it situated?

It is...

- [ ] above a river.
- [x] in the middle of buildings.
- [ ] above a motorway.

GO!

→ Book p. 50

Read the text and comment.

CONSEILS

- Lis le texte. Repère les lieux, les noms propres et les noms de rues.

www.thehighline.org

Walking on the High Line Park is unlike any other experience in New York.

The High Line is a public park built on a historic railway line elevated above the streets on Manhattan's West Side. It runs from Gansevoort Street in the Meatpacking District to West 34th Street, between 10th and 12th Avenues.
On this pathway visitors can take in the sun on lounge chairs, admire the plants or dip their toes during the spring and summer in a water feature.
"The Lawn" is also a popular spot for picnics and summer programs.
Just west of 11th Avenue, the High Line's concrete is transformed into a playground, where children can run, climb and play.

AP ACCOMPAGNEMENT PERSONNALISÉ
DIFFÉRENCIATION

Comment on the text. Choose between the following exercises (A or B).

A

First reading

a. What is the text about?
It is about...
- [x] a public park.
- [ ] a new bridge.
- [ ] a new motorway.

b. It is called...
- [ ] High Line Stadium.
- [x] High Line Park.
- [ ] High Line Avenue.

c. It was...
- [x] an old railway line.
- [ ] an old bridge.
- [ ] an old walking bridge.

Second reading

d. Where is it situated?
It is in...
- [ ] Chinatown.
- [ ] Little Italy.
- [x] Manhattan.

e. It is...
- [x] above the streets.
- [ ] near Central Park.
- [ ] between 5th and 7th Avenues.
- [x] between 10th and 12th Avenues.

Third reading

f. What can people do?
Tick the correct answers.

People can...
- [ ] go swimming.
- [x] sunbathe.
- [x] watch summer programs.
- [x] have a picnic.
- [ ] play baseball.
- [x] enjoy the plants.

Children can...
- [ ] sleep and eat.
- [x] run, climb and play.

B

First reading

a. The text is about a public park.

b. What's its name?

It is called the High Line Park.

c. What was it before?

It was an old railway line.

Second reading

d. Where is it situated?

It is situated in Manhattan's West Side, above the streets, between 10th and 12th Avenues.

5 High Line Park

Third reading

e. What can people do?

People can take in the sun on lounge chairs, admire the plants, dip their toes in a water feature, have a picnic or watch/attend summer programs.

CONSEILS

- Lis le texte avec attention.
- Toutes les réponses aux questions s'y trouvent !
- Après la correction des activités, relis le texte et fais une liste de mots que tu comprends désormais.

Vocabulary

- **mo**torway
- **land**scape
- a**bo**ve

6 Chinatown

GET READY! → Book p. 51

Look and react.

1. What can you see on the first photo?

In the foreground I can see...

- [ ] men and a big dinosaur.
- [ ] men and a big elephant.
- [x] men and a big colorful dragon.

In the background I can see... [x] many people and skyscrapers. [ ] many people in a park. [ ] buildings.

2. What are the people doing on the second photo?

They are...

- [ ] visiting Chinatown.
- [x] shopping.
- [ ] going to the cinema.

3. What do you think the photo represents?

It represents...

- [x] people's everyday life in Chinatown.
- [x] typical grocery shops in Chinatown.
- [ ] restaurants.

GO! VIDEO 9 → Book p. 51

1. Before watching the video do the following exercise. Match the words to their synonyms.

CONSEILS

Cet exercice de vocabulaire va t'aider à anticiper la vidéo.

1. chaotic	a. incredible
2. fascinating	b. all sorts of
3. a store	c. true
4. authentic	d. a shop
5. traditional	e. merchandise
6. unbelievable	f. uncontrolled
7. a range of	g. negociate
8. goods	h. captivating
9. bargain	i. conventional

2. Now watch the video and comment. Choose between the following exercises (A or B).

ACCOMPAGNEMENT PERSONNALISÉ AP

DIFFÉRENCIATION

A

First viewing

a. What is the video about?

It is...

- [ ] a trailer for a new movie.
- [x] a documentary on Chinatown.
- [ ] a cartoon.

b. Who is speaking?

- [ ] A man.
- [x] A woman.

Second viewing

c. What can you find there?

Tick the correct answers.

- [x] Stores.
- [ ] A park.
- [x] Restaurants.
- [x] Grocery store.
- [ ] A station.

d. Some restaurants are...

- [ ] more conventional and classical than in Manhattan.
- [x] more authentic and traditional than in Manhattan.

Third viewing

e. You can buy...

- [ ] "I love London" tee-shirts.
- [ ] "I love Paris" tee-shirts.
- [x] "I love New York" tee-shirts.

f. You can also buy...

- [ ] cellphones.
- [x] DVD players, CDs and stereos.
- [ ] computers.

g. To buy things in Chinatown, you must be...

- [x] good at bargaining.
- [ ] good at English.
- [ ] good at cooking.

B

First viewing

a. What is the video about?

The video is a documentary on Chinatown / a report on Chinatown.

b. Who is speaking in the video?

A woman/a journalist is speaking.

Second viewing

c. What can you find there? Complete the sentences with the words below:
goods / fascinating / restaurants / chaotic / stores

This area is a unique, chaotic and fascinating mix of restaurants and small stores where I can find all sorts of goods .

d. Tick the correct answers.

Some restaurants are like...

- [x] most of the Chinese take-away restaurants in Manhattan.
- [ ] most of the Chinese take-away restaurants in China.

But some restaurants are...

- [ ] more conventional and classical than in Manhattan.
- [x] more authentic and traditional than in Manhattan.

Third viewing

e. What can you buy?

I can buy "I love New York" tee-shirts and a wide range of electronic goods such as DVD players, CDs or stereos..

CONSEILS

Concentre-toi sur les mots que tu connais déjà et repère les mots de l'exercice précédent pour t'aider à comprendre.
Lis bien les questions qui te sont posées avant d'y répondre et garde-les en tête lorsque tu visionnes la vidéo.

Vocabulary

- **neigh**bourhood
- **mos**t of
- in the **fo**reground
- in the **back**ground

PREPARE YOUR FINAL TASKS

→ Book p. 51

Speak about Chinatown. Speak about the things you can see, the things you can do or buy there.

Chinatown is a neighbourhood in New York ... There is/are... There you can...

CONSEILS

Utilise :
1. *There is / there are* pour dire ce qui se trouve dans le quartier.
2. Le comparatif pour comparer ce quartier à d'autres qui te plaisent moins.
3. *Can* + BV pour dire ce que tu peux y faire / y acheter.

L'expression du futur avec *will* + BV → Book p. 53

Pour parler de l'avenir j'utilise ....will.... + ...BV.... .

Attention : ....will.... est ....invariable...., il n'y a donc pas de « ....s.... » à la 3e personne du singulier.

1 Remets les mots dans l'ordre.

a. New York / will / in / the / I / of / Statue / Liberty / see.

I will see the Statue of Liberty in New York.

b. in / New York / will / I / visit / the Empire State Building.

In New York, I will visit the Empire State Building.

c. go / you / will / to / Coney Island / ?

Will you go to Coney Island?

d. my / will / parents / Rockefeller Center / visit / the.

My parents will visit the Rockefeller Center.

e. sister / not / will / my / go / Ellis Island / to / she / see / to / wants / Chinatown.

My sister will not go to Ellis Island, she wants to see Chinatown.

2 Écris des phrases pour dire ce que tu feras ou ne feras pas l'été prochain.

go to the beach / swim / surf / sunbathe / visit Paris / eat ice cream / drink cocktails / windsurf / go to New York / go scubadiving / visit museums / ride a bike / ride a horse.

Next summer, I will go to the beach and I will surf but I will not visit Paris! I will swim and sunbathe but I will not visit museums...

Les adjectifs composés → Book p. 53

Pour former ....un adjectif composé.... je garde en tête qu'il est ....invariable....

et que ....le trait d'union.... est ....obligatoire.... !

3 **Relie le début de chaque phrase avec la fin qui lui correspond.**

1. Stephen Wiltshire is ...
2. Stephen's panorama of New york is ...
3. The George Washington Bridge is ...
4. Paris to New York? It is ...
5. Stephen's cityscape of New York is ...

a. a six-meter cityscape.
b. a 604-foot-high bridge.
c. a forty-eight-hour job.
d. an eight-hour-long flight.
e. a forty-three-year-old artist.

4 **Fais des phrases à partir des éléments donnés en utilisant les adjectifs composés.**

a. Going from Brooklyn to Manhattan is a *(three / hours)* walk.

Going from Brooklyn to Manhattan is a three-hour walk.

b. The Statue of Liberty is approximately a *(130 / years / old)* sculpture.

The Statue of Liberty is approximately a 130-year-old sculpture.

c. It is a *(93 / meters / high)* statue.

It is a 93-meter-high statue.

Le comparatif de supériorité → Book p. 53 et 54

Pour comparer deux éléments entre eux j'utilise le comparatif .

Pour les adjectifs courts (1 ou 2 syllabes) :

adjectif court + er + than

Pour les adjectifs longs :

more + adjectif long + than

Attention: -y devient « -ier » !

Ex. : tiny → tin ier

Exceptions :
good → better

bad → worse

5 **Mets les adjectifs courts entre parenthèses au comparatif de supériorité.**

a. The Statue of Liberty is (low) lower than the Empire State Building.

b. Traffic? It is (crazy) crazier in New York City than in Paris!

c. The Statue of Liberty is a little (old) older than the Eiffel Tower.

d. Times Square is (noisy) noisier than Ellis Island.

e. The World Trump Tower is (small) smaller than the One World Trade Center.

6 Mets les adjectifs longs entre parenthèses au comparatif de supériorité.

a. New York City is (cosmopolitan) more cosmopolitan than Los Angeles.

b. The monuments in New York are (impressive) more impressive than in any other American city.

c. Chinatown is (extensive) more extensive than Greenwich Village.

7 Compare les éléments qui te sont proposés avec un adjectif de ton choix.

a. The Brooklyn Bridge (1825 m) / the Golden Gate Bridge (2737 m).

The Brooklyn Bridge is more beautiful/is shorter than the Golden Gate Bridge.

b. The Empire State Building (381 m) / the Chrysler Building (319 m)

The Empire State Building is taller/more elegant than the Chrysler Building.

c. Central Park / High Line Park

Central Park is larger/more majestic than High Line Park.

Le modal *can* → Book p. 54

Pour exprimer une possiblité ou une impossibilité j'utilise :

can / can't + BV .

Tout comme will, can est invariable, il ne prend pas de « s »

à la 3e personne du singulier.

8 Explique ce que tu peux faire au High Line Park de New York. Utilise *can* + BV.

a. Celebrate Halloween each October with the ghosts of the High Line.

You can celebrate Halloween each October with the ghosts of the High Line.

b. Learn about the High Line's history, its design, public art program and unique horticulture.

You can learn about the High Line's history, its design, public art program and unique horticulture.

c. Experience the High Line through music and motion, from dance parties to the beat of Latin rhythms.

You can experience the High Line through music and motion from dance parties to the beat of Latin rhythms.

d. Enjoy quiet mornings on the park with weekly Tai Chi and Meditation sessions.

You can enjoy quiet mornings on the park with weekly Tai Chi and Meditation sessions.

Language practice PHONOLOGY

L'accentuation des adjectifs composés → Book p. 54 41 CD1 41 MP3

1 Écoute les mots suivants et entoure la syllabe accentuée.

a. A ten-meter-long street.

b. A two-story house.

c. A five-year-old building.

d. A twenty-minute ride

e. A 200-meter avenue.

f. a two-day trip.

Le son [ɪ] et le son [iː] → Book p. 54 43 CD1 43 MP3

Complète la règle à l'aide des mots suivants : bref / long / énergique / insiste.

Le son [ɪ] est un son bref et énergique comme dans « **li**ve ».

Le son [iː] est un son long sur lequel on insiste comme dans « **lea**ve ».

2 Écoute les mots suivants et classe-les dans la bonne colonne.

hit / beach / weekend / little / beachgoers / immediate / picnic / ice cream / bring / it / with.

[iː]		[ɪ]	
beach	immediate	hit	immediate
weekend	ice cream	little	bring
beachgoers		picnic	with / it

Auto-évaluation

→ Book p. 58

Connaissances et compétences linguistiques

Vocabulary

- Je connais le vocabulaire de la ville.
- Je connais le vocabulaire utilisé pour décrire un monument.

Grammar

- Je sais utiliser *will*+ BV pour parler de l'avenir.
- Je sais utiliser les adjectifs composés.
- Je sais utiliser le comparatif de supériorité.
- Je sais utiliser le modal *can*.

Phonology

- Je sais accentuer les adjectifs composés.
- Je sais faire la différence entre le son [i:] et le son [ɪ].

Compétences langagières et domaines du socle commun

Écouter et comprendre
Domaines 1, 2

- Je sais comprendre les points essentiels d'une vidéo.
- Je sais comprendre un interview.

Lire et comprendre
Domaines 1, 2

- Je sais lire et comprendre les points essentiels d'un texte informatif.

Parler en continu
Domaines 1, 2, 3

- Je sais décrire un monument ou un quartier à l'oral.
- Je sais raconter ce qui se passe dans une vidéo.

Écrire
Domaines 1, 2

- Je sais rédiger un commentaire sur un monument / sur une ville.

Réagir et dialoguer
Domaines 1, 2, 3

- Je sais exprimer mes goûts et opinions sur un monument / un quartier.

PEAC

Culture et Parcours
Domaines 1, 2, 3, 5

- Je connais les principaux monuments de New York.
- Je connais le style architectural de certains monuments.
- Je sais me repérer sur un plan de New York.

4 Once upon a time...

1 A fairy tale

GET READY!

→ Book p. 60

Look at the document and answer the questions.

1. Describe what you see.

a. I can see...

- ☑ two characters and a fruit.
- ☐ two women and seven giants.
- ☐ a princess, a witch and magic creatures.

b. What fruit do you recognize?

- ☐ An orange.
- ☑ An apple.
- ☐ A banana.

2. Guess what fairy tale it is.

It is...

☐ Cinderella. ☐ Beauty and the Beast. ☑ Snow White and the seven dwarves.

GO!

→ Book p. 60

Read and write.

CONSEILS

- Tu ne vas sans doute pas tout comprendre au texte, mais essaie de repérer les sujets pour trouver les personnages.

Once upon a time[1] there lived a lovely princess with fair skin and blue eyes. She was[2] so fair that she was named Snow White. Her mother died when Snow White was a baby and her father married again. This queen was very pretty but she was also very cruel. The wicked stepmother[3] wanted to be the most beautiful lady in the kingdom[4] and she often asked her magic mirror, "Mirror! Mirror on the wall! Who is the fairest of them all?" And the magic mirror always said, "You are, Your Majesty!" But one day, the mirror replied, "Snow White is the fairest of them all!" The wicked queen was very angry and jealous of Snow White. She ordered her huntsman[5] to take Snow White to the forest and kill her...

www.shortstoriesshort.com

1. il était une fois – 2. prétérit de *be* – 3. belle-mère – 4. royaume – 5. chasseur

Read and comment on the text.
Choose between the following exercises (A or B).

ACCOMPAGNEMENT PERSONNALISÉ AP
DIFFÉRENCIATION

A

First reading

a. Pick out the characters. How many characters are there in the text?

There are... ☐ 2. ☑ 3. ☐ 4. ☐ 5.

b. Who are the main characters?

☐ A king. ☑ A princess. ☑ A queen. ☐ A prince. ☑ A huntsman. ☐ A witch.

Second reading

c. Find the 9 adjectives in the text then fill in the grid.

Physical description	Personality	Others
fair, pretty, beautiful.	lovely, cruel, wicked,	magic.
	angry, jealous.	

d. Match the adjectives to the corresponding characters.

fair, pretty, lovely. — cruel, wicked, angry, jealous, pretty, beautiful. — magic.

Third reading

e. What happened? Complete the sentence with the following words: kill / beauty / beautiful / jealous / her.

The Princess was so beautiful that the Queen was jealous of her beauty and wanted to kill her.

B

First reading

a. Pick out the characters. How many characters are there? There are 3 characters.

b. Who are the characters in this fairy tale?

They are a princess, a queen and a huntsman.

c. What is the princess's name? The princess's name is Snow White.

Second reading

d. Find the 9 adjectives in the text then fill in the grid.

Physical description	Personality	Others
fair, pretty, beautiful.	lovely, cruel, wicked,	magic.
	angry, jealous.	

e. Match the adjectives to the corresponding characters.

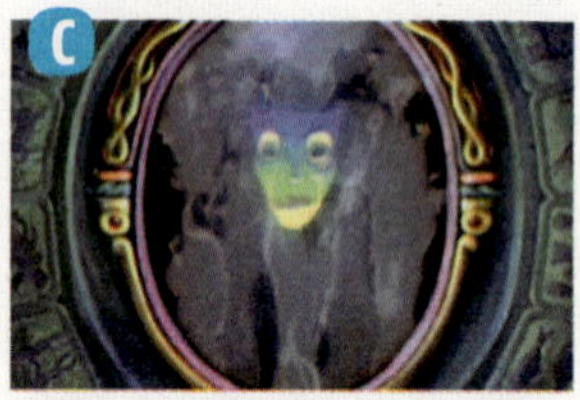

fair, pretty, lovely. cruel, wicked, angry, jealous, pretty, beautiful. magic.

Third reading

f. What happened? Why was the princess named "Snow White"?

She was named "Snow White" because her skin was very fair.

g. Say why Snow White had a stepmother.

She had a stepmother because her mother died and her father remarried.

h. Say what the queen's problem was. The queen was jealous of Snow White's beauty.

i. Say what the queen decided to do. She decided to kill Snow White.

CONSEILS

Lis le texte trois fois au moins et repère les mots que tu connais, les mots transparents (qui s'écrivent de la même façon en français et en anglais), et ceux qui ressemblent au français.

Vocabulary

- **w**icked
- fair
- once u**pon** a time
- **step**mother

2 A new version

GET READY!

→ Book p. 61

Look at the document and answer the questions.

1. Say who you recognize.

a. The woman is...

- [ ] Jasmine.
- [x] Snow White.
- [ ] Little Red Riding Hood.

b. Who are the people around her?

They are...

- [x] the seven dwarves.
- [ ] her brothers.
- [ ] her classmates.

c. Match their names to the correct picture.

Bashful / Doc / Dopey / Grumpy / Happy / Sleepy / Sneezy

2. How does the woman look?

She looks... [ ] tired. [ ] worried. [x] happy.

GO! VIDEO 10 → Book p. 61

Watch and comment on the video. Choose between the following exercises (A or B).

AP ACCOMPAGNEMENT PERSONNALISÉ

DIFFÉRENCIATION

A

First viewing

a. Say everything you can about the document. Identify the characters and tick the ones you see.

- [x] The seven dwarves.
- [x] Snow White.
- [ ] The prince.
- [ ] The huntsman.
- [ ] The queen.
- [x] A witch.

b. Where are the characters?

- [ ] At the beach.
- [ ] At the castle.
- [x] In the forest.
- [ ] In the mountain.

c. This document is...

- [ ] a teaser.
- [x] an advertisement.
- [ ] a film.
- [ ] a football match.

Second viewing

d. Say what you understand about the story. Say why the wicked queen was angry.

The Evil Queen was mad with...

- [ ] mercy
- [ ] pity
- [x] envy/jealousy

of Snow White's beauty.

e. What did the Queen do then?

- [ ] She decided to change her hairstyle.
- [x] She transformed herself into an old woman.
- [ ] She visited a fashion designer.

f. She offered Snow White...

- [ ] an apple pie.
- [ ] a bowl of cereals.
- [x] a poisoned apple.

Third viewing

g. Say what Snow White asks. Complete the missing word.

Is it ...organic...?

h. What do you think about the end of the video?

I think it is funny...

because Snow White refuses

to eat the apple.

She only eats organic fruit!

CONSEILS

- Regarde la vidéo attentivement.
- Repère les différences entre l'histoire
- de la première leçon et cette vidéo.
- Repère les personnages.

CONSEILS
- Concentre-toi sur l'histoire.
- De quel type de document s'agit-il ?
- Que peux-tu dire de la fin ?

B

First viewing

a. Say everything you can about the document. Who are the characters?

The characters are the seven dwarves and Snow White.

b. Where are the characters? They are in the forest.

c. Is this document a film, a football match or an advert/advertisement?

It is an advert/advertisement.

Second viewing

d. Say what you understand about the story. The Evil Queen was driven mad with...

envy/jealousy of Snow White's beauty.

e. What did the Queen transform herself into?

She transformed herself into an old woman.

f. What did she give Snow White?

She gave Snow White a poisoned apple.

Third viewing

g. Say what Snow White asks. Complete the missing word."Is it organic ?"

h. What is the Queen's reaction? She is angry/furious.

i. What do you think about the end of the video?
I think it is funny because Snow White refuses to eat the apple. She only eats organic fruit!

PREPARE YOUR FINAL TASKS

→ Book p. 61

Write about the similarities and differences between the video and the original Snow White story.

In the video, Snow White was... In the original story she was...

CONSEILS
- Relis le texte de l'histoire de Snow White (leçon 1), puis regarde à
- nouveau la vidéo. Fais une liste des différences et des points communs.
- Puis rédige tes phrases en reprenant le vocabulaire des leçons.

Vocabulary
- an **ad**vertisement / **ad**vert
- **hunts**man
- **en**vy
- **jea**lousy
- mad
- **poi**soned

3 Jack and the Beanstalk

GET READY! → Book p. 62

Read and react.

Once upon a time, there lived a widow[1] woman with her son, Jack, and Bessie the cow on their small farm in the country. Every day, Jack would help his mother with the chores[2]. But despite[3] all their hard work, Jack and his mother were very poor. "What shall we do, what shall we do?" said the widow. "We must sell our cow, Old Bess."

1. veuve – 2. corvées – 3. malgré

1. Read the text and match the characters with their names.

- Bessie
- Jack
- The widow (Jack's mother)

2. Say what you understand.

a. The boy and his mother lived...
- [ ] in a castle in the forest.
- [x] on a farm in the country.
- [ ] in a house in the city.

b. Jack...
- [ ] never helped his mother with the housework.
- [x] always helped his mother with the housework.

c. Jack and his mother...
- [x] did not have any money.
- [ ] had a lot of money.

d. So they decided to...
- [ ] sell their house.
- [x] sell their cow.

GO! → Book p. 62 49 CD1

Listen and comment on the audio. Choose between the following exercises (A or B).

AP ACCOMPAGNEMENT PERSONNALISÉ — DIFFÉRENCIATION

CONSEILS

- Essaie d'abord de repérer le sens global de ce que tu écoutes. Ensuite concentre-toi sur les mots que tu connais pour t'aider à comprendre.

A

First listening

a. Listen and say what you understand about the story. Right or wrong?

- Jack and his mother were very rich. R / (W)
- Jack's mother wanted to sell her cow. (R) / W
- On his way to the market, Jack met an old man. (R) / W
- The old man gave him a lot of money for the cow. R / (W)
- Jack planted the beans in the garden. R / (W)

Second listening

b. Describe the situation. Put the sentences in the correct order.

- A man gave Jack magic beans in exchange for the cow. 3
- Jack and his mother were not rich, they only had a cow. 1
- Jack's mother was furious and threw the magic beans outside. 4
- Jack went to the market to sell the cow. 2

Third listening

Talk about the magical event in the story.

c. The beans transformed themselves into...

- ☐ a new cow.
- ☑ a giant beanstalk.
- ☐ money.

d. What did Jack do?

He...

- ☑ started to climb on the giant beanstalk.
- ☐ was really scared.
- ☐ applauded.

B

First listening

a. Listen and say what you understand about the story.
Right or wrong? When it's wrong, correct the sentence.

Jack and his mother were very rich. Wrong. Jack and his mother were very poor.

Jack's mother wanted to sell her cow. Right

On his way to the market, Jack met an old man. Right

The old man gave him a lot of money for the cow. Wrong. The old man gave him magic beans.

Jack planted the beans in the garden. Wrong. Jack's mother threw the beans out.

Second listening

b. Describe the situation.
Put the sentences in the correct order.

- A man gave Jack magic beans in exchange for the cow. 3
- Jack and his mother were not rich, they only had a cow. 1

3 Jack and the Beanstalk

– Jack's mother was furious and threw the magic beans outside. 4

– Jack went to the market to sell the cow. 2

Third listening

Talk about the magical event in the story.

c. What did Jack's mother do with the beans? She threw the beans out of the window.

d. When Jack looked out of the window, he saw a giant beanstalk.

e. What was the magical element? The beans were the magical element.

CONSEILS

- Pendant tes écoutes, essaie de noter les mots que tu connais.
- Concentre-toi sur les mots accentués, ils sont porteurs de sens.
- Tu peux comprendre les informations essentielles d'un texte audio sans nécessairement comprendre tous les mots.

Vocabulary

- farm
- plant
- throw **out**
- sell

4 Jack and the giant

GET READY! → Book p. 63

Read and write.

1. Identify the people and the places.

a. At the top of the beanstalk, Jack...

☑ discovered a castle and went in.

☐ discovered a little house and went in.

b. There, he saw...

☑ a giant. ☐ a dwarf.

Jack climbed the beanstalk and saw a beautiful castle. He went inside. Then he heard a loud voice: "Fee! Fi! Fo! Fum!" Jack hid in a cupboard[1]. A huge[2] giant came in. On the table were a hen[3] and a gold harp. The hen laid an egg of gold for the giant and the harp sang a song. The giant fell asleep. Jack took the hen and the harp and ran. But the harp called for help. The giant awoke and chased Jack down[4] the beanstalk.

1. placard - 2. immense - 3. poule - 4. pourchasser

2. What happened?

a. On the table there were...

☐ a cat and a dog sleeping.

☑ a gold harp and a hen.

b. What did they do?

☑ They laid an egg and sang a song.

☐ They meowed and barked.

c. The giant... ☐ sang along. ☑ fell asleep.

3. Say what Jack took from the giant.

a. Jack took...

☐ the magic beans.

☑ the harp and the hen.

☐ some chicken and chips.

b. Then, he...

☐ started eating them.

☑ ran away.

GO! 51 CD1 → Book p. 63

Listen and comment on the audio. Choose between the following exercises (A or B).

ACCOMPAGNEMENT AP PERSONNALISÉ
DIFFÉRENCIATION

CONSEILS
- Écoute le document audio. Note les mots que tu ne comprends pas. Si besoin, réécoute le début de l'histoire.

A

First listening

a. What dit Jack do? Write the correct number in the square brackets.

- [2] The angry giant woke up.
- [4] The giant followed Jack down the beanstalk.
- [1] Jack ran away with the hen and the harp.
- [3] Jack went down the beanstalk.

Second listening

b. What happened at the end of the story? Tick the correct answer.

- [ ] Jack gave the hen and the harp back to the giant.
- [ ] Jack chopped the beanstalk and the giant fell down.
- [✓] Jack's mother chopped the beanstalk and the giant crashed to the ground.

Third listening

c. Speak about Jack and his mother. Jack and his mother...

- [ ] ate the magic beans.
- [✓] lived happily ever after with the hen and the harp.
- [ ] sold the hen and the harp.

B

First listening

a. What did Jack do? Put the sentences in the correct order. Be careful, there are mistakes!

Write the correct number in the square brackets.

- [2] The angry giant woke up.
- [ ] The giant grabbed Jack and threw him in the cupboard.
- [4] The giant followed Jack down the beanstalk.
- [ ] Jack fell from the beanstalk and crashed on the ground.
- [1] Jack ran away with the hen and the harp.
- [3] Jack went down the beanstalk.

Second listening

b. What happened at the end of the story?

Jack's mother chopped the beanstalk and the giant crashed to the ground.

CONSEILS
- Intéresse-toi aux personnages. Identifie-les. Ensuite, note les différentes étapes de l'histoire. Sois très attentif.

Vocabulary
- **cup**board
- a hen
- huge
- chase down

4 Jack and the giant

Third listening

c. Speak about Jack and his mother.

Jack and his mother lived happily ever after with the hen and the harp.

CONSEILS

Réécoute l'histoire de Jack et relis tes réponses. Reprends tes notes et essaie de résumer la fin de l'histoire. Ne fais pas de phrases trop compliquées. Tu dois utiliser le prétérit.

PREPARE YOUR FINAL TASKS → Book p. 63

Tell the end of the story in your own words.

The giant came down after Jack...

5 Little Red Riding Hood – Part 1

GET READY! → Book p. 64

1. What is the girl wearing?

a. Look at the picture. Match the names with the objects.

a cloak / an umbrella / a basket / a hood

b. What is she wearing? She is wearing a red cloak with a hood.

c. What is she carrying? She is carrying a basket.

2. What is in the basket? Why?

a. In the basket, there is/are... ☐ books. ☑ food. ☐ her shopping.

b. She is taking it to... ☐ her mother. ☐ her grandfather. ☑ her grandmother.

c. Now give the name of the girl. She is Little Red Riding Hood.

GO! → Book p. 64

Read and comment on the text. Choose between the following exercises (A or B).

AP – ACCOMPAGNEMENT PERSONNALISÉ
DIFFÉRENCIATION

In came the little girl in red.
She stopped. She stared[1]. And then she said,
"What great big ears you have, Grandma".
"All the better to hear you with", the Wolf replied.
"What great big eyes you have, Grandma."
said Little Red Riding Hood.
"All the better to see you with", the Wolf replied.
He sat there watching her and smiled.
He thought, I'm going to eat this child.
Compared with her old Grandmamma,
She's going to taste like caviar.
Then Little Red Riding Hood said,
"But Grandma, what a lovely great big furry coat[2]
you have on".

Roald Dahl, *Little Red Riding Hood and the Wolf*, 1982.

1. fixa - 2. manteau de fourrure

CONSEILS

Lis le texte trois fois. Repère les mots que tu connais. Tu as certainement déjà lu une autre version de cette histoire. Essaie de t'en souvenir et de repérer les différences.

A

First reading

a. What sort of document is it?

☐ A text in a newspaper. ☑ A tale. ☐ A detective story.

b. Say who wrote the story and when.

Roald Dahl wrote the story in 1982.

c. Give the complete name of the story.

Little Red Riding Hood and the Wolf.

d. Read the list of verbs in the infinitive form below.
Find the corresponding preterite in the text and say if they are regular (R) or irregular (IR) verbs.
come / stop / stare / reply / sit / say / think

Preterit:

came (IR) – stopped (R) – stared (R) – replied (R) – sat (IR) – said (IR) – thought (IR)

Second reading

e. Find the expressions from the original story: underline the expressions which are in the text.

– What a lovely great big furry coat you have on!

– What big teeth you have!

– What great big feet you have!

– What a big nose you have!

– What great big ears you have!

– What great big eyes you have!

Third reading

f. Read from line 9 to line 14. Right or wrong?

– The Wolf was not happy to see Little Red Riding Hood. Wrong

– Little Red Riding Hood was in danger. Right

– The Wolf wanted to eat Little Red Riding Hood. Right

– The Wolf thought she would not be good to eat. Wrong

– Little Red Riding Hood was scared of the Wolf. Wrong

– She thought the Wolf had a beautiful furry coat on. Right

Vocabulary

- all the **be**tter
- **no**tice **some**thing

B

First reading

a. What sort of document is it? It is a tale.

b. Say who wrote the story and when. Roald Dahl wrote the story in 1982.

c. Give the complete name of the story. *Little Red Riding Hood and the Wolf.*

d. Find all the verbs in the preterite in the text.

came – stopped – stared – replied – sat – said – thought.

e. Write the infinitive form of the verbs and say if they are regular (R) or irregular (IR) verbs.

come (IR) – stop (R) – stare (R) – reply (R) – sit (IR) – say (IR) – think (IR)

Second reading

f. Read the expressions below and find the expressions which are in the text.

– What a lovely great big furry coat you have on!

– What big teeth you have!

– What great big feet you have!

– What a big nose you have!

– What great big ears you have!

– What great big eyes you have!

Third reading

g. Read from line 9 to 14 and answer the questions.

– What did the Wolf want to do? He wanted to eat her.

– What did he think about Little Red Riding Hood? He thought she is going to taste like caviar.

– What did Little Red Riding Hood notice about the Wolf?

She noticed that he had great big eyes, great big ears and a lovely furry coat.

– Was Little Red Riding Hood scared? No, she wasn't. She was surprised.

CONSEILS

- Lis le texte avec attention, repère les personnages.
- Qui parle ? Sous quelle forme est le texte ?

6 Little Red Riding Hood – Part 2

GET READY!

→ Book p. 65

1. Look at the picture and react.

a. Match the names with the corresponding arrows.
the wood / a furry coat / an eyelid / the small girl.

b. Who is this girl?

- ☐ Snow White.
- ☑ Little Red Riding Hood.
- ☐ Little Red Riding Hood's grandmother.

2. Where is she?

She is...

- ☐ at her grandmother's house.
- ☑ in the forest.

3. What clothes is she wearing now?

She is wearing...

- ☑ a furry coat.
- ☐ a dress.
- ☐ a red cloak with a hood.

GO! → Book p. 65

Read and comment on the text.

Then Little Red Riding Hood said,
"But Grandma, what a lovely great big furry
coat you have on."
"That's wrong!" cried Wolf.
"Have you forgot
To tell me what BIG TEETH I've got?
Ah well, no matter what you say,
I'm going to eat you anyway."
The small girl smiles. One eyelid flickers[1].
She whips[2] a pistol from her knickers[3].
She aims it at the creature's head,
And bang bang bang, she shoots him dead[4].
A few weeks later, in the wood,
I came across Miss Riding Hood.
But what a change! No cloak of red,
No silly hood upon her head.
She said, "Hello, and do please note
My lovely furry wolfskin coat."

Roald Dahl, *Little Red Riding Hood and the Wolf*, 1982.

1. elle cligne de l'œil
2. elle sort
3. slip
4. elle le tue d'un coup de revolver

CONSEILS

Lis le texte au moins trois fois. Repère les mots et les noms que tu connais. Sois attentif à la sonorité des mots, ils t'aideront à comprendre la forme du texte. Pour t'aider tu peux lire le texte à haute voix. Note tous les mots que tu ne comprends pas. Essaie de te souvenir de l'histoire originale

Choose between the following exercises (A or B).

AP Accompagnement personnalisé – Différenciation

A

First reading

a. What can you say about this document? It is the ......second...... part of the tale.

b. After reading part 1 and part 2, can you identify the document?
It is... [ ] a poem. [ ] a tale. [x] both: a tale and a poem.

c. Who are the two main characters in this part?
- [ ] Little Red Riding Hood and her grandmother.
- [x] The Wolf and Little Red Riding Hood.
- [ ] The Wolf and Little Red Riding Hood's grandmother.

Second reading

d. Say what you understand. Underline the correct answers.

– Did Little Red Riding Hood say "What big teeth you've got" to the Wolf?

Yes, she did. / No, she said "What a lovely great big furry coat you have on".

– Did the Wolf eat Little Red Riding Hood? Yes, he did. / No, he didn't.

– Did Little Red Riding Hood die? Yes, she died. / No, she did not die.

– Did she survive? Yes, she survived. / No, she didn't survive.

– Did she shoot the Wolf? Yes, she shot the Wolf. / No, she did not shoot him.

– Did she kill the Wolf? Yes, she killed the Wolf. / No, she didn't kill the Wolf.

– Did she buy a new coat? Yes, she bought a new coat. / No, she didn't buy a new coat.

– Did she make herself a furry wolfskin coat? Yes, she made herself a furry wolfskin coat. / No, she did not make herself a furry wolfskin coat.

Third reading

e. Describe the end of the story.

It is... ☐ similar to the original ending of the tale.
☑ different from the original ending of the tale.

f. Tick the correct answers to justify your choice.

☑ Little Red Riding Hood shot the Wolf.
☐ The Wolf shot Little Red Riding Hood.
☑ The Wolf died.
☐ Little Red Riding Hood died.
☐ Little Red Riding Hood made herself a new basket.
☑ Little Red Riding Hood made herself a wolfskin coat.

g. In this version, Little Red Riding Hood is...

☐ scared. ☑ brave. ☐ sad.

B

First reading

a. What can you say about this document? It is the second part of the tale.

b. After reading part 1 and part 2, is this text a poem, a tale or both (a poem and a tale)? It is both: a poem and a tale.

c. Who are the two main characters in this part?

The main characters are Little Red Riding Hood and the Wolf.

Second reading

d. Say what you understand. Answer these questions and give details when you can.

– Did Little Red Riding Hood say "What big teeth you've got" to the Wolf?

No, she didn't, she said "What a lovely great big furry coat you have on".

CONSEILS

Lors de tes lectures, repère les personnages. Sont-ils les mêmes que dans la première partie ? Quelle est la différence avec le conte classique ?

– Did the Wolf eat Little Red Riding Hood? No, he didn't eat her.

– Did Little Red Riding Hood die? No, she didn't die.

– Did she survive? Yes, she did / Yes, she survived.

– Did she shoot the Wolf? Yes, she did / Yes, she shot the Wolf.

– Did she kill the Wolf? Yes, she did / Yes, she killed the Wolf.

– Did she buy a new coat? No, she didn't buy a new coat.

– Did she make herself a furry wolfskin coat?

Yes, she made herself a furry wolfskin coat.

Third reading

e. Describe the end of the story. Is the end of the tale similar to or different from the original ending?

It is different from the original ending of the tale.

f. Justify your choice by ticking the correct answers.

- [x] Little Red Riding Hood shot the Wolf.
- [ ] The Wolf shot Little Red Riding Hood.
- [x] The Wolf died.
- [ ] Little Red Riding Hood died.
- [ ] Little Red Riding Hood made herself a new basket.
- [x] Little Red Riding Hood made herself a wolfskin coat.

g. In this version, is Little Red Riding Hood scared, brave or happy?

She is not scared, she is brave.

Vocabulary

- **kni**ckers
- both
- **sca**red
- one **eye**lid flickers
- whip
- shoot him dead

PREPARE YOUR FINAL TASKS

→ Book p. 65

Rewrite this tale (part 1 and part 2) in your own words.

Little Red Riding Hood came to visit her grandmother but...

She stopped and said...

The Wolf wanted...

Little Red Riding Hood didn't say...

CONSEILS

Pour réécrire ce conte avec tes propres mots, tu peux utiliser les verbes suivants au prétérit : *came / found / stopped / wanted / said / killed / shot / survived / made herself*. Tu peux aussi utiliser la forme négative.

Le prétérit simple régulier → Book p. 67

Le prétérit correspond à notre passé composé, notre imparfait ou notre passé simple.

C'est le temps du récit, celui utilisé dans les contes.

Sa formation est très simple pour les verbes réguliers :

→ BV + *-ed*

1 Conjugue les verbes entre parenthèses au prétérit.

a. Once upon a time, a king and a queen (live) lived in a beautiful castle.

b. They (name) named their daughter Snow White.

c. But Snow White's mother (die) died.

d. d. Her father (remarry) remarried an evil queen.

Le prétérit irrégulier → Book p. 67

Rappel : les verbes irréguliers ne suivent pas la règle des verbes réguliers :

tu dois <u>les apprendre par cœur</u>. → voir le tableau des verbes irréguliers

2 Imagine ce que le Petit Chaperon Rouge a pu dire après avoir tué le loup et mets les verbes entre parenthèses au prétérit.

a. What great big ears he (have)! What great big ears he had!

b. But he (eat) my Grandma! But he ate my Grandma!

c. What a lovely great big furry coat I (wear)! What a lovely great big furry coat I wore!

d. The red hood (not / be) my style at all! The red hood was not my style at all!

Le prétérit à la forme interrogative → Book p. 67

Dans les *Yes / No questions*, j'utilise ....did........ + Sujet + ...BV........ .

Ex.: ....Did........ he ....eat........ Little Red Riding Hood?

Dans les questions ouvertes (*Wh-*), je mets un ....mot interrogatif........ devant ....did........ .

Ex.: ....Where........ ....did........ Little Red Riding Hood ....go........ ?

3 Imagine une question possible aux réponses suivantes.

a. Her mother died when Snow White was a baby. When did Snow White's mother die?

b. Snow White only ate organic apples. What did Snow White eat?

c. No, Jack and his mother did not have a lot of money. Did Jack and his mother have a lot of money?

d. Jack climbed up the beanstalk. What did Jack climb up?

Le prétérit à la forme négative → Book p. 68

Au prétérit simple, la forme négative se construit avec :

........did........ + ...not........ + ...BV........ .

Attention, la marque du prétérit est déjà sur l'auxiliaire ....did........, donc le verbe est à l'infinitif !

4 Mets ces phrases à la forme négative avec *did not* + BV.

a. Little Red Riding Hood / say "what great big teeth you have".

Little Red Riding Hood didn't say "what great big teeth you have".

b. The Wolf / reply "the better to eat you with my dear".

The Wolf didn't reply "the better to eat you with, my dear".

c. The Wolf / eat Little Red Riding Hood.

The Wolf didn't eat Little Red Riding Hood.

d. The Huntsman / save Little Red Riding Hood and her grandmother.

The Huntsman didn't save Little Red Riding Hood and her grandmother.

Language practice PHONOLOGY

La prononciation de *-ed* → Book p. 68

Quand le verbe se termine par « t » ou « d », on prononce [id].

Quand le verbe se termine par [p], [k], [f], [s], [ʃ], [ʧ], on prononce [t].

Pour tous les autres cas, on prononce [d].

1 Écoute les verbes suivants et dis si tu entends [t], [d] ou [id]. Écris chaque verbe dans la bonne colonne. 56 CD1 54 MP3

died / loved / hunted / walked / asked / invited

[t]	[d]	[id]
asked	died	hunted
walked	loved	invited

L'intonation dans les *Yes/No questions* et dans les questions en *–Wh* au prétérit → Book p. 68 58 CD1 56 MP3

2 Écoute les questions suivantes et dis si la voix monte ou descend.

a. What did Little Red Riding Hood say to the Wolf?
b. Did the Wolf eat Little Little Red Riding Hood?
c. What did she do?

Auto-évaluation

Connaissances et compétences linguistiques

Vocabulary

- J'ai mémorisé le vocabulaire pour écrire un conte.
- J'ai mémorisé les titres des contes traditionnels en anglais.
- J'ai mémorisé les noms des animaux et des personnages dans les contes.

Grammar

- Je sais utiliser le prétérit régulier et irrégulier en anglais aux formes affirmative, négative et interrogative.

Connaissances et compétences linguistiques

Phonology

- Je sais prononcer les trois prononciations possibles de *-ed*.
- Je connais l'intonation montante et descendante des *Yes/No questions* et des questions en *Wh-* au prétérit.

Compétences langagières et domaines du socle commun

Écouter et comprendre
Domaines 1, 2

- Je peux comprendre un message oral pour réaliser une tâche (A1).
- Je peux comprendre les points essentiels d'un document oral sur un sujet connu ou familier en lien avec les thèmes culturels du programme (le conte).
- Je sais repérer à l'oral les personnages, les lieux.

Lire et comprendre
Domaines 1, 2

- Je peux comprendre des textes courts et simples en relevant des noms, des mots familiers, en relisant si nécessaire (A1).
- Je peux saisir la trame narrative d'un récit sur un sujet familier ou déjà connu (relevant des thèmes culturels du programme) (A2).
- Je sais lire et comprendre le résumé très simple d'un conte.
- Je sais lire et comprendre l'essentiel d'une poésie adaptée d'un conte.

Parler en continu
Domaines 1, 2, 3

- Je sais parler des personnages de contes étudiés en classe.
- Je sais décrire des images, des dessins sur les contes.
- Je sais présenter un conte seul et en groupe.

Écrire
Domaines 1, 2, 5

- Je sais reformuler de façon simple un conte et en écrire la suite.
- Je sais écrire un dialogue simple.

Réagir et dialoguer
Domaines 1, 2, 3

- Je sais échanger des informations sur les contes étudiés en classe.
- Je sais dialoguer avec un camarade pour finaliser une présentation.
- Je sais communiquer en groupe pour élaborer une production commune.

PEAC

Culture et Parcours
Domaines 1, 2, 3, 5

- Je découvre des contes de la littérature britannique.
- Je connais les contes principaux du monde anglo-saxon et leur place dans la littérature, le cinéma, les arts, la publicité.

5 Crazy about fashion

1 Dressed by the kids

GET READY!

→ Book p. 74

Look at the documents and do the exercice.

Match the correct number to the pictures.

number 1: The children are dressing up like stars.

number 2: The man is wearing a cardboard box.

number 3: The little girl is putting a tiara on her father's head.

number 4: The mum is pretending to be a superhero.

number 5: The mum and her kid are smiling.

GO!

→ Book p. 74

Read the text and do the following exercices.

1. Underline the words you know and circle the ones you don't know.

Adapted from: www.t-g.com

My mom is just fine with the way she dresses but I would like to see my dad have long brown hair. My dad has to wear the same thing every day so I would like to see him in a tuxedo[1]. Maybe bright orange.

My mom has blonde hair so I would dye it brown so she would look like everyone else in the family because we all have brown hair! Or just for fun, I would like to see my mom with blonde hair and red stripes running through it!

(Mason Wright, 12 years old)

1. smoking

CONSEILS

Lis attentivement le texte. Repère les mots en rapport aux vêtements, aux couleurs, etc.

ACCOMPAGNEMENT PERSONNALISÉ AP

DIFFÉRENCIATION

2. Comment on the text. Choose between the following exercises (A or B).

A

First reading

a. Who is writing?
- [x] A boy.
- [ ] A girl.

b. What's his name?
- [ ] Mason Right.
- [x] Mason Wright.
- [ ] Mason White.

c. How old is he?

He is...
- [x] 12.
- [ ] 14.
- [ ] 11.

Second reading

d. Who and what is he talking about?
- [ ] His sister.
- [x] His parents.
- [ ] His clothes and look.
- [x] His parents' looks.

e. Who does he want to makeover?
- [ ] His brother.
- [x] His dad.
- [x] His mother.

Third reading

f. What would he like to change? He would like to see his father...
- [ ] in an orange jacket.
- [x] in an orange tuxedo.
- [ ] in a blue tuxedo.

g. With...
- [ ] short blonde hair.
- [x] long brown hair.
- [ ] short auburn hair.

h. He would like to see his mother with...
- [ ] red hair and blonde stripes.
- [x] blonde hair and red stripes.
- [x] brown hair.

B

First reading

a. Who is writing?

A boy is writing.

b. What's his name?

His name is Mason Wright.

c. How old is he?

He is 12.

Second reading

d. Who and what is he talking about?

He is talking about his parents and their clothes and looks.

e. Who does he want to makeover?

He wants to makeover his mother and his father.

Third reading

f. What would he like to change?

He would like his father to have this look:
- [x] Long brown hair and a bright orange tuxedo.
- [ ] Short blonde hair and sportswear clothes.
- [ ] Curly auburn hair and a suit.

g. He would like his mother to have this look:
- [ ] Red hair and blonde stripes.
- [x] Brown hair.
- [x] Blonde hair and red stripes.

CONSEILS

- Lis attentivement les questions de la grille choisie. Aide-toi du vocabulaire donné puis réponds aux questions. Toutes les réponses sont dans le texte.

Vocabulary

- same = identical
- bright = brilliant
- stripes = bands of different colors
- through
- dye: *teindre*

2 On the catwalk

GET READY! → Book p. 75

Look at the documents and do the following exercises.

1

2

3

4

1. Look at the photos and comment on their styles. Write the number of the picture under the correct words.

black trousers / a black and green striped mini skirt / a black tee-shirt / a dark bow tie / a green sweater /

2 … 4 … 4 … 1 … 2

red trousers / a purple jacket / a white and red tee shirt / a dark coat / a green tie / black socks /

3 … 4 … 1 … 3 … 3 … 4

khaki trousers / a yellow and blue sweater / a tweed jacket / a dark scarf / a colourful jumper

1 … 1 … 1 … 2 … 3

2. What are they wearing? Tick the correct answer.

a. The boy with the glasses is wearing... ☑ khaki trousers. ☐ black trousers.

b. He has got... ☐ a blue sweater. ☑ a tweed jacket and a dark bow tie.

c. The girl with the black woolly hat is wearing...
☐ pink trousers, a yellow shirt, a blue sweater, a brown jacket and a red scarf.
☑ black trousers, a blue shirt, a green sweater, a yellow jacket and a black scarf.

3. Which outfit do you like best?

a. I prefer the boy wearing... ☐ red trousers and a tie. ☐ a bow tie and glasses.

b. I prefer the girl with... ☐ the hat and the yellow jacket. ☐ the black and green striped skirt and the purple jacket.

GO! VIDEO 11 → Book p. 75

Watch and react.

Comment on the video. Choose between the following exercises (A or B).

AP ACCOMPAGNEMENT PERSONNALISÉ

DIFFÉRENCIATION

CONSEILS

- Tu vas regarder la vidéo trois fois. À chaque fois, sois très attentif à ce qui se passe. Il y a de nombreux personnages. Note ce que tu vois au fur et à mesure.

A

First viewing (0.00 min to 0.29 min)

a. Who can you see at first?
- ☐ A boy and a girl.
- ☑ A teenager and a little girl.
- ☐ A teenager and a boy.

b. Where are they?
☐ At school. ☐ At home. ☑ In a library.

c. What is the video about?
- ☐ A movie.
- ☑ A fashion show for a charity.
- ☐ A concert.

d. Whose fashion show is it?
☐ Dior's. ☐ Chanel's. ☑ Ralph Lauren's.

e. What are the people doing?
- ☑ They are dressing up the children.
- ☑ They are putting make-up on the children.
- ☐ They are acting in a film.
- ☑ They are taking photos.
- ☐ They are dancing.

Second viewing (0.29 min to the end)

f. The girl with a blue skirt and a white jumper is carrying...
- ☐ a dog.
- ☑ a fluffy toy.
- ☐ a bag.

g. The boy with the tie looks...
- ☑ very elegant.
- ☐ sad.
- ☐ messy.

h. What are the two girls doing in the corridor?
- ☑ Skateboarding.
- ☐ Dancing.
- ☐ Reading.

i. Name all the different kinds of clothes you can see.

Shoes / skirt / trainers / boots / tie / jacket / hat / jumper / trousers / tee shirt / sweater.

Third viewing

j. Write as many sentences as you can to comment on the show.

Everybody is having fun. There are a lot of people. The clothes look beautiful. They are all wearing nice outfits.

CONSEILS

- Pour répondre aux questions, pense à utiliser tout le vocabulaire travaillé. Note la couleur des vêtements que tu vois, sois attentif aux différents détails de la vidéo.

B

First viewing (0.00 min to 0.29 min)

a. Who can you see at first? I can see a girl and a teenager.

b. Where are they? They are in a library.

c. What is the video about? It's a fashion show for a charity.

d. Whose fashion show is it? Ralph Lauren's.

e. What are the people doing?

They are dressing up the children; they are putting make-up on the children; they are taking photos.

Second viewing (0.29 min to the end)

f. What is the girl with a blue skirt and a white jumper carrying?

The girl with a blue skirt and a white jumper is carrying a fluffy toy.

g. How does the boy with the tie look like?

The boy with the tie looks very elegant and smart.

h. What are the girls with the white outfits doing?

They are skateboarding.

i. Name all the kinds of clothes you can.

Shoes / skirt / trainers / boots / tie / jacket / hat / jumper / trousers / tee shirt / sweater

j. Describe the two girls with the skateboard.

The girl with the orange hat is skating on a yellow skateboard.

The girl with the black hat is skating on a pink skateboard.

They are wearing flashy clothes.

They are having fun.

k. What are the girls with the white outfits doing?

The girls with the white outfits are dancing / having fun / messing around.

Third viewing

l. Write as many sentences as you can to comment on the show.

PREPARE YOUR FINAL TASKS

→ Book p. 75

Watch the video again, choose one outfit and make 5 sentences to describe it.

The boy with the... is wearing a nice... / The girl carrying a... has a beautiful...

Vocabulary

- **fluffy** toys
- **take selfies**
- **have** fun
- look **happy**
- pull **faces**
- **dance**
- en**joy**

CONSEILS

Pour réaliser ton commentaire, tu dois :

1. Décrire qui tu es et où tu es.
   a. *Te présenter : "Hello, this is... reporting for..."*
   b. *Présenter l'événement : "We are in..., at... fashion show..."*
   c. *Décrire les mannequins et les vêtements : "... is coming now, she is wearing..."*
2. Exprimer tes sentiments sur la tenue que tu as choisie.
   "Her dress is too...!"
3. Parler de la couleur des vêtements, de la matière...
4. Finir ton commentaire.
   "See you next... at..."

3 London fashion

GET READY!

→ Book p. 76

1. Who and what can you see? Circle the words corresponding to the picture.

classic / different / original / hairstyle / punk / flashy / market / shop / colourful / funny-looking / boring / a man / sad / simple / colourless / ordinary / conventional / two women.

2. Say what the persons are wearing. Tick the correct answers.

a. The woman in front is wearing...

- [x] a flashy pink and blue dress.
- [ ] black jeans and a green tee shirt.

b. Describe her.
- [x] She has colourful hair.
- [ ] She has got blond hair.
- [ ] She looks very classical.
- [x] She is funny-looking.

c. The man standing is wearing...
- [x] black and red trousers.
- [ ] dark green jeans.

d. Describe him.
- [ ] He has got a blue sweater.
- [x] He has got a beige tee shirt and a green checkered shirt.
- [x] He is wearing red shoes.
- [ ] He is wearing black boots.

e. The woman with blond hair is wearing...
- [ ] a black skirt and a red tee shirt.
- [x] a red and blue skirt, a black tee shirt and black tights.

f. Describe her.
- [x] She has got sandals and a long necklace.
- [ ] She has got high heels and earrings.

g. The man sitting is wearing...
- [x] red checkered trousers.
- [ ] a yellow vest.

h. Describe him.
- [x] He has got a funny hairstyle.
- [x] He has got purple hair.
- [ ] He is dressed in black.

CONSEILS

Essaie d'abord de repérer le sens global de la vidéo en t'aidant des images. Ensuite, concentre-toi sur les mots que tu connais pour t'aider à construire du sens. Sois attentif au lieu qui est décrit. Prends des notes sur ce que tu vois.

GO! VIDEO 12 → Book p. 76

Comment on the video. Choose between the following exercises (A or B).

AP ACCOMPAGNEMENT PERSONNALISÉ — DIFFÉRENCIATION

A

First viewing

a. The video is...
- [ ] a cartoon.
- [x] a report.
- [ ] news.

b. The video is about...
- [x] Camden Lock.
- [ ] Camden Tock.
- [ ] Camden Block.

Second viewing

c. When can people come to Camden Lock?

They can come...
- [ ] on weekends.
- [x] every day.
- [ ] during the week.

d. Why do they come there?

They come because of...
- [ ] the river.
- [ ] the supermarket.
- [x] the stores, the stalls and the market.

Third viewing

e. Comment on the different fashion styles.

In Camden Lock you can find different fashion styles such as...
- [x] grunge.
- [x] punk.
- [ ] classic.
- [x] retro.
- [ ] hipster.
- [x] gothic.

B

First viewing

a. What sort of video is it?

It is...

- [ ] a TV series.
- [ ] a documentary.
- [x] a report.

b. Who present the video?

- [ ] A man.
- [x] A journalist.
- [x] A woman.

c. What is the video about?

The video is about Camden Town and its market called Camden Lock.

Second viewing

d. When can people come to Camden Lock?

They can come seven days a week/every day. It is open all year round.

e. Why do they come there?

They come because of the stores, the stalls and the market.

f. What fashion styles can you find there? Tick the correct answers.

- [x] Grunge.
- [x] Punk.
- [ ] Classic.
- [x] Retro.
- [ ] Hipster.
- [x] Gothic.

Third viewing

g. Comment on the different fashion styles.

Describe the couple at the end of the video (01.07'). What is their fashion style?

The man is wearing jeans and a blue and grey coat. He has got a small hat. He is wearing dreadlocks.

The woman is wearing a blue skirt with a shiny belt, a leopard coat and a woolly hat. She has got pink hair. She is carrying a brown handbag.

I think they have a grunge style because they look very cool.

CONSEILS

Avant de répondre aux questions, lis-les très attentivement. Réfléchis aux différents styles vestimentaires que tu as vu dans la vidéo, que tu connais et que tu aimes. Note les mots que tu ne comprends pas et n'hésite pas à poser des questions lors de la mise en commun.

Vocabulary

- **dread**locks = a hairstyle worn in the Rastafarian style with long matted curls
- stalls = market space for a specific activity
- **shin**y = bright/glossy
- **ca**rry = transport something

4 Mo's bows

GET READY! → Book p. 77

Look at the picture and answer the questions.

1. Who can you see?

a. Who are the two people on the photo?

They are Mo and Barack Obama.

b. Who is Barack Obama?

- ☐ The British Prime Minister.
- ☐ A famous actor.
- ☑ The President of the USA from 2008 to 2016.

c. Guess where they are.

- ☐ At Mo's house.
- ☐ At Mo's school.
- ☑ At the White House, in the President's office.
- ☑ In the Oval Office.

2. Who do you think Mo is?

☐ Barack Obama's son. ☑ A young designer. ☐ Barack Obama's assistant.

What does he make? He makes bow ties.

3. What can you see on the desk? Circle the right picture.

I can see bow ties on the desk.

tie

bow tie

scarf

GO! VIDEO 13 → Book p. 77

Watch and comment on the video. Choose between the following exercises (A or B).

ACCOMPAGNEMENT PERSONNALISÉ AP
DIFFÉRENCIATION

CONSEILS
- Regarde la vidéo. Sois attentif à ce que dit Mo. Concentre-toi sur les images pour comprendre la situation.

A

First viewing

a. What is Mo's complete name?

His complete name is Moziah Bridges.

b. Who does he live with?

- [x] His mother.
- [ ] His grandmother.
- [ ] His sister.
- [x] His cousin Taylor.
- [x] His dog Spiro.
- [x] His aunt.

Second viewing

c. What does he do for a living?
He is...

- [x] a CEO.
- [x] a designer.
- [ ] an employee.
- [ ] a popstar.

d. CEO stands for...

- [x] Chief Executive Officer.
- [ ] Central European Organization.

e. What is the name of his company?

The name of his company is "Mo's bows".

f. How many bow ties does he own?

- [ ] 100.
- [x] 200.
- [ ] 300.

Third viewing

g. Who helped him make bow ties at first?

- [x] His grandmother.
- [ ] His mum.
- [ ] His aunt.

h. What is Mo's motivation?
He wants to...

- [ ] make people smile.
- [x] make people happy.
- [ ] make people like fashion.
- [ ] make people more elegant.
- [ ] make people sad.

B

First viewing

a. What is Mo's complete name? His complete name is Moziah Bridges.

b. Who does he live with? He lives with his mum, his aunt, his cousin and his dog.

c. Give the name of his cousin. His cousin's name is Taylor.

d. Give the name of his dog. His dog's name is Spiro.

CONSEILS

Lis d'abord les questions puis regarde plusieurs fois la vidéo. Aide-toi du vocabulaire vu. Repère les mots-clefs et note-les dans ton cahier.

Second viewing

e. What does he do for a living? He makes bow ties.

f. He is the CEO of his company means...
- ☑ He owns the company.
- ☑ He is the boss.
- ☐ He is an employee.

g. CEO stands for...
- ☑ Chief Executive Officer.
- ☐ Central European Organization.

h. Give the name of his company. The name of his company is "Mo's bows".

Third viewing

i. How many bow ties does he own? He owns 200 bow ties.

j. Who helped him make bow ties at first? His grandmother.

j. What is Mo's motivation?

He believes he can make people happy.

k. Give your opinion about Mo.

I think he is intelligent and funny/clever and nice.

CONSEILS

Sois original dans ta description. Fais un croquis au crayon et note tous les termes que tu veux utiliser pour décrire ton nœud papillon. Reprends le vocabulaire que tu as vu dans la leçon et celui de la vidéo. Utilise *made of* pour décrire ta création.

Vocabulary

- **nice**
- **clever** = intelligent
- means = method used to obtain something
- own = possess
- mean = have sense

PREPARE YOUR FINAL TASKS

→ Book p. 77

Draw your favourite bow tie and describe it to your classmates. Then show your drawings. Which one is the most original?

Look at my drawing... My bow tie is made of...

5 Fashion for all

GET READY! → Book p. 78

Look and react.

1. Who do you see?

a. On the two photos I can see...
- [x] two young women.
- [ ] two girls.

b. What's their job?
- [ ] They are actresses.
- [ ] They are journalists.
- [x] They are fashion models.

c. Because...
- [x] they are wearing nice dresses.
- [ ] they are presenting the news on TV.
- [ ] they are in a cinema studio.

d. How do they look?
- [ ] They look sad.
- [x] They look happy.
- [ ] They look tired.

e. What is special about them?
- [ ] They are fat.
- [x] They suffer from a disease.
- [ ] They are not American.

2. What can you say about these two women?

a. Do you think they like their job?

Yes, I do because they look happy on the photo / because they are smiling / because they are really beautiful.

b. Do you think their life is easy or difficult? Explain.

I think their life is difficult because they suffer from a disease / because they are different / because it is not easy to look different.

I think their life is easy because they are certainly rich / because they certainly have a lot of friends.

c. Is it a good thing that Chantelle and Madeline are models?

Yes, it is because they are beautiful. They are examples for people suffering from a disease. It proves they can do what they want.

GO!

→ Book p. 78

1. These words will help you understand the interview. Link the synonyms.

a. way	1. a candidate
b. life-time	2. incomparable
c. profound	3. manner
d. unique	4. deep
e. a contestant	5. for an entire life

(a – 3; b – 5; c – 4; d – 2; e – 1)

9 CD2 **2. Now listen to the interview of Chantelle Brown-Young.**

3. Comment on the interview. Choose between the following exercises (A or B).

AP ACCOMPAGNEMENT PERSONNALISÉ — DIFFÉRENCIATION

A

First listening

a. Give information about Chantelle. How old is she?

She is...

- [ ] eighteen years old.
- [x] nineteen years old.
- [ ] twenty-nine years old.

b. What country and what city is she from?

She is from...

- [ ] Montreal, Canada.
- [ ] Ottawa, Canada.
- [x] Toronto, Canada.

Second listening

c. What is her dream?

- [ ] She wants to be America's youngest model.
- [x] She wants to be America's next top model.

Third listening

d. Why is she unique?

She is unique because...

- [ ] she knows many fashion designers.
- [x] her story is painted on her body.
- [ ] she is very famous.

B

First listening

a. Give information about Chantelle. How old is Chantelle? She is 19 (nineteen) years old.

b. What country and what city is she from? She is from Toronto, Canada.

Second listening

c. What is her dream? She wants to be America's next top model.

Third listening

d. Why is she unique? She is unique because her story is painted on her body.

CONSEILS

Écoute attentivement l'interview. Concentre-toi sur les mots-clefs et sur les mots que tu reconnais. Chantelle répond à plusieurs questions que tu n'entends pas dans l'audio. Pour t'aider, note les différentes étapes de cet interview : *"First, she says", "Then, she wants...", "Her dream is..."*.

Vocabulary

- **dis**ease = illness
- **ama**zing
- **bra**ve = courageous

6 Fashion history

GET READY! → Book p. 79

1. Look at the couple and react. Match the words with the photos.

a dress / high heel shoes / a blazer / jeans / trousers / a bow tie / a long-sleeved shirt / a handbag / a necklace / trainers / a hat / a leather jacket / gloves.

1925

gloves
a dress
high heel shoes
a hat
a bow tie
a long-sleeved shirt
a blazer
trousers

1955

a necklace
a handbag
a leather jacket
jeans
trainers

2. Say what they were wearing.

On the first picture, the woman is wearing a long dress, a hat, gloves and high heel shoes.

The man is wearing beige trousers, a blue blazer, a white shirt, a bow tie and a hat.

GO! VIDEO 14 → Book p. 79

Watch and comment on the video. Choose between the following exercises (A or B).

AP ACCOMPAGNEMENT PERSONNALISÉ
DIFFÉRENCIATION

CONSEILS

Regarde plusieurs fois la vidéo.
Attention, il n'y a pas de dialogue, il faut donc te concentrer sur les images !

A

First viewing

a. What sort of document is it?
- [x] A video.
- [ ] A cartoon.
- [ ] An extract from a book.

b. The man and the woman are...
- [ ] journalists.
- [ ] teachers.
- [x] models.

Second viewing

c. What are the couple doing? The man and the woman...
- [ ] are sleeping.
- [x] are changing clothes.
- [ ] are working.

d. The video shows...
- [ ] different fashion styles in the 19th century.
- [x] changes in fashion over 100 years.

e. It goes from...
- [x] 1915 to 2015.
- [ ] 1925 to 2005.

Third viewing

f. – Compare what the couple were wearing and in 1915 and in 2015.
– In 1915, the couple were wearing...
– In 2015, the couple were wearing...

B

First viewing

a. What sort of document is it?
It is... [ ] a trailer for a movie. [ ] a cartoon. [x] a documentary.

b. Who can you see?
[x] A man and a woman. [ ] A football team. [ ] Two reporters.

Second viewing

c. What are the couple doing?
[ ] They are dancing. [x] They are trying clothes on. [ ] They are eating.

d. Why are they doing that?
[ ] Because they are hungry. [ ] Because they are happy. [x] To show different clothes over the century.

CONSEILS

Lis bien les questions et sois très attentif. Fais attention aux détails des différentes tenues et aux époques. Pour répondre, utilise le vocabulaire vu et entendu.

Third viewing

e. Say what they were wearing in 1915 and in 2015.

– In 1915, the man was wearing beige trousers, a beret and a checkered jacket.

– In 2015, the woman was wearing jeans, high heels, a leather jacket and jeans.

PREPARE YOUR FINAL TASKS

→ Book p. 79

You are going to a fancy dress party. You must choose a style from the past. Describe the outfit you are wearing.

I'm wearing a 1975 outfit. It is...

CONSEILS

- Regarde à nouveau la vidéo pour choisir ton style.
- N'oublie pas d'utiliser *be* + *ing* pour décrire ta tenue.
- Pense également à utiliser des adjectifs (couleur, matière...).

Vocabulary

- top = piece of clothing for the upper body
- belt: *une ceinture*
- **pre**tty = lovely
- **hand**some = good-looking
- **che**ckered = marked with squares

Language practice GRAMMAR

Le modal *would* → Book p. 81

Pour exprimer un souhait, je peux utiliser would like to + BV.

1 Construis des phrases avec *would like*.

a. She / buy a Chanel dress.

She would like to buy a Chanel dress.

b. They / go to the New York's fashion week.

They would like to go to the New York's fashion week.

c. My parents / wear casual clothes at work.

My parents would like to wear casual clothes at work.

L'exagération → Book p. 81

On marque l'exagération en utilisant : too + adj.

Too much + nom indénombrable.

Too many + nom dénombrable pluriel.

2 Complète les phrases suivantes par l'adjectif qui convient dans la liste ci-dessous :

transparent / small / long

a. This dress is too long for her, she is walking on the hem!

b. This blouse is too transparent, I refuse to wear it!

c. I am too small, I can't see the podium!

3 Complète les phrases avec *too much* ou *too many*.

a. There are too many people here, we cannot see anything.

b. This coat costs too much money, I can't afford it!

c. This fashion show takes too much time, it's boring!

Le présent *be + V-ing*

Lorsque l'on utilise ....le présent.... pour décrire une personne (ses vêtements, ses activités), il faut conjuguer ....be.... et ajouter ....ing.... à la base verbale.

4 Utilise le présent en *be + V-ing* pour compléter les phrases suivantes.

a. In the video the couple (change) ....are changing.... clothes.

b. They look very happy and they (smile) ....are smiling.... .

c. They (have) ....are having.... fun.

5 Construis des questions en utilisant les mots donnés.

Ex.: the woman / hold / a purse → Is the woman holding a purse?

a. the man / wear / a tie / a hat / and

Is the man wearing a tie and a hat?

b. the man / the woman / wear / a hat / and

Are the man and the woman wearing a hat?

c. she / hold / handbag / wear / sunglasses

Is she holding a handbag and wearing sunglasses?

L'exclamation → Book p. 82

J'utilise ....What a/an + adjectif + nom singulier ou pluriel.... pour marquer l'exclamation.

6 Fais des phrases exclamatives à l'aide de *what* (*a/an*) + adjectif.

Ex.: She is wearing an amazing dress. → What an amazing dress she is wearing!

a. He is wearing an incredible bow. What an incredible bow he is wearing!

b. Mo is organizing a huge show for his presentation. What a huge show Mo is organizing!

c. Mo has supportive parents. What supportive parents Mo has!

Le superlatif → Book p. 82

J'utilise le superlatif pour dire ....le plus, la plus.....

Avec un adjectif court, j'utilise ....the + adj + est.... .

Avec un adjectif long, j'utilise ....the most + adj.... .

Lorsqu'un adjectif se termine par -y, il se transforme en ....-iest.....

Les exceptions sont : good → ....the best.... bad → ....the worst....

7 Complète les phrases avec le superlatif qui convient.

a. This is (good) ....the best.... fashion show I have ever seen.

b. Chantelle is (incredible) ....the most incredible.... model tonight.

c. (Difficult) ....The most difficult.... thing is the way people look at you when you are different!

Language practice PHONOLOGY

L'intonation des questions → Book p. 82

La voix ....descend.... dans une question en *Wh-*.

La voix ....monte.... dans les *Yes/No questions*.

1 Écoute les réponses ci-dessous, rédige les questions et note si la voix monte ou descend. 12 CD2 67 MP3

a. Yes, I would love to go to London. Would you love to go to London? ↗

b. I would like to buy a shirt in Camden. What would you like to buy in Camden? ↘

c. He would like to become a model. What would he like to become? ↘

d. No, she wouldn't want to have blue hair. Would she want to have blue hair? ↗

L'accentuation de l'exclamation → Book p. 82

2 Éoute les phrases suivantes et note l'accentuation. 14 CD2 69 MP3

a. He is making bow ties.

b. What fantastic creations Mo has designed!

c. Barack Obama loves Mo's designs.

d. What a good-looking boy he is!

Auto-évaluation

Connaissances et compétences linguistiques

Vocabulary

- J'ai mémorisé le vocabulaire des vêtements.
- J'ai mémorisé le vocabulaire du monde de la mode.

Grammar

- Je sais dire ce que j'aimerais faire en utilisant le modal *would*.
- Je sais utiliser la structure de l'exagération.
- Je sais utiliser la structure de l'exclamation.
- Je sais utiliser le superlatif.
- Je sais utiliser le présent *be* + V-*ing* et je sais prononcer le -*ing*.

Phonology

- Je sais prononcer les phrases exclamatives avec la bonne intonation.

Compétences langagières et domaines du socle commun

Écouter et comprendre
Domaines 1, 2
- Je sais comprendre les informations essentielles d'un interview.
- Je sais écouter et comprendre les informations d'une vidéo ou d'un reportage.

Lire et comprendre
Domaines 1, 2
- Je sais comprendre les informations essentielles d'un texte court.

Parler en continu
Domaines 1, 2, 3
- Je sais décrire les images d'un défilé de mode.
- Je sais rendre compte d'un interview ou d'un reportage.
- Je sais commenter un défilé de mode.

Écrire
Domaines 1, 2
- Je sais écrire des phrases simples pour décrire les vêtements que portent les mannequins.

Réagir et dialoguer
Domaines 1, 2
- Je sais communiquer en groupe pour élaborer une production commune.

PEAC

Culture et Parcours
Domaines 1, 2, 3, 5
- J'ai découvert le monde de la mode anglo-saxonne.

6 Long to reign over us

1 Long live the Queen!

GET READY!

→ Book p. 88

Look at the document and answer the questions.

1. Who is this document about?

- [ ] It is about French monarchs.
- [x] It is about British monarchs.
- [ ] It is about Spanish monarchs.

2. Give information about the kings and queens mentioned in the document. Tick the correct answers.

- [x] Elizabeth II became queen in 1952.
- [x] Elizabeth II is the longest reigning monarch.
- [ ] Elizabeth II's great-great-grandmother Queen Victoria became queen in 1840.
- [ ] George III was king for 58 years.
- [ ] Queen Victoria is the shortest reigning monarch.
- [x] Queen Victoria was queen for 63 years.
- [x] Charles II died in 1685.
- [ ] Queen Victoria died 300 years ago.

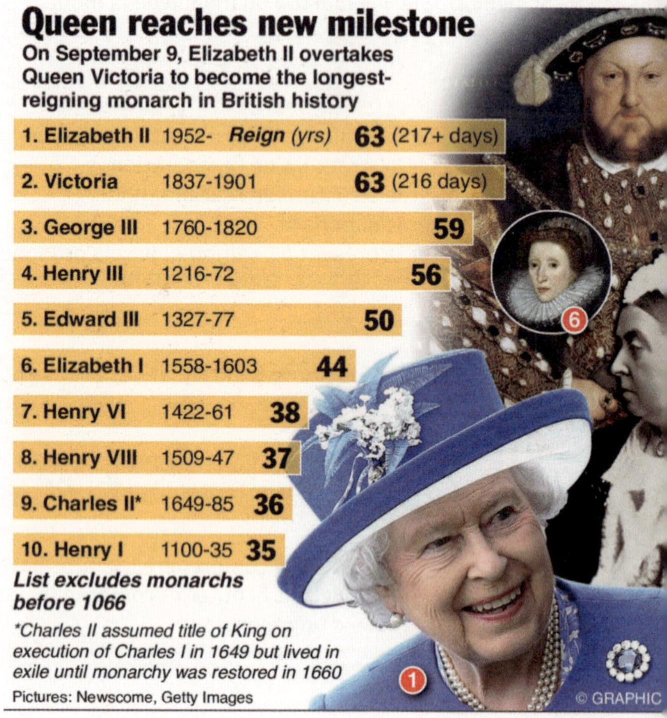

GO!

→ Book p. 88

Read and write.

Longest Reigning UK Monarch

Queen Elizabeth II is set to become[1] the longest reigning monarch in British history. On Wednesday, she will beat[2] the record set by her great-great-grandmother, Queen Victoria, who reigned for 63 years and 7 months. Only four other British kings and queens have sat[3] on the throne for 50 years or more. At 89 years old, Queen Elizabeth is still active and makes public appearances. Palace officials say there will be no major celebrations for the historic day, simply "business as usual", at the Queen's request. "The British by and large[4] really rather[5] love her and certainly respect her enormously", said royal historian Hugo Vickers.

www.timeforkids.com, September 8th 2015.

1. s'apprête à devenir – 2. battre – 3. se sont assis – 4. dans l'ensemble – 5. plutôt

CONSEILS

- Sois attentif à toutes les dates, aux chiffres et aux noms propres. Repère les mots transparents et note ceux que tu ne comprends pas.

Read and comment on the text.
Choose between the following exercises (A or B).

ACCOMPAGNEMENT PERSONNALISÉ AP
DIFFÉRENCIATION

Vocabulary
- great-great-**grand**mother

A

First reading

a. What can you say about this document?
- [x] It is an article.
- [ ] It is a cartoon.
- [ ] It is a letter.

b. What is the publication date?
- [x] September 8th 2015.
- [ ] September 18th 2015.
- [ ] October 18th 2015.

c. It is about...
- [ ] King Henry VI.
- [ ] Queen Elizabeth I.
- [x] Queen Elizabeth II.

Second reading

d. Give information about the Queen. How old is she in the article? She is...
- [ ] fifty years old.
- [ ] sixty-three years old.
- [x] eighty-nine years old.

e. She is...
- [ ] the shortest reigning British monarch.
- [x] the longest reigning British monarch.

f. Except for Queen Elizabeth, how many British monarchs reigned for fifty years or more?
- [x] 4
- [ ] 5
- [ ] 6

Third reading

g. What is she like?
- [ ] She is not very active.
- [ ] She is not active anymore.
- [x] She is active.

h. She does not make any public appearances because she is very old.
Right / (Wrong)

i. How do British people feel about the Queen?
- [ ] They don't like her.
- [x] They love her.
- [x] They respect her.

CONSEILS
- Fais bien attention aux chiffres et aux dates qui se trouvent dans le texte !
- Relis les questions attentivement.

B

First reading

a. What can you say about this document?

It is an article.

b. What is the publication date?

It is September 8th 2015.

c. Who is it about?

It is about Queen Elizabeth II.

Second reading

d. Give information about the Queen. How old is she in the article?

She is eighty-nine years old.

e. She is...
- [ ] the shortest reigning British monarch.
- [x] the longest reigning British monarch.

f. Except for Queen Elizabeth, how many British monarchs reigned for fifty years or more?

Four British monarchs reigned for fifty years or more.

Third reading

g. What is she like?

She is still active.

h. Does she make some public appearances?

Yes, she does.

i. How do British people feel about the Queen?

They really rather love her and respect her enormously.

2 90 years in pictures

GET READY! → Book p. 89

Look at the document and answer the questions.

1. What is this document about?

a. This document is… ☑ a timeline. ☐ a photograph. ☐ a cartoon.

b. It is… ☐ Queen Elizabeth I's timeline. ☐ Queen Victoria's timeline. ☑ Queen Elizabeth II's timeline.

2. Make sentences about the important dates of this person's life.
Don't forget to use the preterit.

a. Queen Elizabeth / become / Queen / 1952 / her coronation / take place / 1953.

Queen Elizabeth became Queen in 1952 and her coronation took place in 1953.

b. She / celebrate / her Silver Jubilee / 1977.

She celebrated her Silver Jubilee in 1977.

c. 2002 / mark / the Golden Jubilee of her reign.

2002 marked the Golden Jubilee of her reign.

d. She / celebrate / her Diamond Jubilee / 2012.

She celebrated her Diamond Jubilee in 2012.

e. She / turn / 90 years old / 2016.

She turned 90 years old in 2016.

GO! 15 VIDEO → Book p. 89

Watch and react. Comment on the video.
Choose between the following exercises (A or B).

ACCOMPAGNEMENT PERSONNALISÉ AP
DIFFÉRENCIATION

CONSEILS
Attention ! Il n'y a pas de paroles. Sois attentif aux dates. N'hésite pas à revoir la vidéo plus de trois fois.

A

First viewing

a. What can you say about the Queen? Give her name.

Her name is Queen Elizabeth II.

b. In the first picture…
- [x] she is a baby.
- [ ] she is a teenager.
- [ ] she is an old woman.

c. In the last picture…
- [ ] she is a baby.
- [ ] she is a teenager.
- [x] she is an old woman.

d. What does this series of pictures show?
- [x] It shows 90 years of her life.
- [ ] It shows 26 years of her life.
- [ ] It shows 50 years of her life.

Second viewing

e. What are the important dates of her life? Tick the correct answers.
- [x] She had a son, Charles in 1948.
- [ ] She celebrated her 70th birthday in 2016.
- [x] She became Queen in 1952 and her coronation took place in 1953.
- [ ] Queen Elizabeth II was born in Paris.
- [x] She got married to Prince Philip in 1947.
- [x] Later, she had a daughter, Anne and she had two other sons, Andrew in 1960 and Edward in 1964.

Third viewing

f. Give other important information about her. Circle the correct answers.

– At 4 years old, Elizabeth II had a brother / (a sister).

– Her father died (in 1952) / in 2002.

– She (liked) / hated riding horses with young Prince Charles.

– In 1973, she had (three dogs) / three cats.

– She met Nelson Mandela in 1965 / (1995) and Angelina Jolie in 1994 / (2014) but she also met American Presidents, French Presidents, sportsmen, British Prime ministers…

B

First viewing

a. What can you say about the Queen? Give her name.
- [ ] Her name is Queen Elizabeth I.
- [x] Her name is Queen Elizabeth II.
- [ ] Her name is Princess Elizabeth II.

b. What can you say about the Queen in the first picture? In the first picture, she is a baby.

c. What can you say about the Queen in the last picture? In the last picture, she is an old woman.

d. How many years of the Queen's life do these pictures show? These pictures show 90 years of the Queen's life.

Second viewing

e. What are the important dates of her life? Give the correct answers and dates.

She had a ......son......, Charles in ......1948...... . She celebrated her ......90th birthday...... in 2016. She became Queen in ......1952...... and her coronation took place in 1953. Queen Elizabeth II was born in ......London...... . She got married to ......Prince Philip...... . Later, she had a daughter, ...Anne...... and she had two other sons, ...Andrew...... in ......1960...... and ......Edward...... in ......1964...... .

Third viewing

f. Give other important information about her. Choose Right or Wrong and correct the sentences if necessary.

– At 4 years old, Elizabeth II had a brother. Right / (Wrong)

At 4 years old, Elizabeth II had a sister.

– Her father died in 1952. (Right) / Wrong

....

– She liked riding horses with young Prince Charles. (Right) / Wrong

....

– In 1973, she only had one dog. Right / (Wrong)

In 1973, she had three dogs.

– She met Nelson Mandela in 1995 and Angelina Jolie in 2014 but she also met American Presidents French Presidents, sportsmen, British Prime ministers... (Right) / Wrong

....

PREPARE YOUR FINAL TASKS

→ Book p. 89

Write down Queen Elizabeth's short biography.
Take into account the important dates of her life.

1926 / 1947 / 1948 / 1951 / 1953 / 1983 / 2016

CONSEILS

Pour écrire ton paragraphe, tu peux t'aider de ce que tu as vu dans le manuel et des activités des autres leçons. Reprends le vocabulaire que tu as vu dans les grilles. Tu dois utiliser le prétérit simple.

Vocabulary

- coro**nat**ion
- **Sil**ver **Ju**bilee = 25th anniversary
- **Gol**den **Ju**bilee = 50th anniversary
- **Dia**mond **Ju**bilee = 60th anniversary
- **take place**
- turn **nine**ty

3 New British coin

GET READY!

→ Book p. 90

Look and react.

1. What is it?

obverse

reverse

a. It is...
- [ ] a banknote.
- [x] a coin.
- [ ] a cheque.

b. What is the value of this object?
- [ ] 5 €
- [x] £5
- [ ] $5

c. What currency is it?

It is...
- [x] 5 British Pounds
- [ ] 5 British Euros
- [ ] 5 English Pounds

2. Who do you recognize?
- [ ] Duchess Kate Middleton
- [ ] Queen Elizabeth I
- [x] Queen Elizabeth II

3. What else can you see?

a. Complete the picture with the words "obverse" and "reverse".

b. On the reverse, I can see...
- [ ] a flag, a crown, £5 and 90.
- [ ] four flags, the letters and number EII R and 90.
- [ ] two flags, ER, 90, £5 and a crown.
- [x] four flags, EII R, 90, a crown, a date, £5 and Her Majesty Queen Elizabeth II.

GO!

→ Book p. 90

Read the text and do the following exerices.

www.westminsterinternationalshop.com

New Queen Elizabeth II Coin Issue

This year our Queen became the only British sovereign to celebrate her 90th birthday ever. To celebrate this momentous occasion, a brand new golden coin was issued: The Queen Elizabeth II 90th Birthday £5 Coin. The coin features[1] [...] a 90th birthday portrait of Queen Elizabeth II on the obverse, designed by renowned international sculptor Luigi Badia.

The reverse depicts[2] the union and royal standard flags with 90 at the centre and the royal cypher, above, encircled by the words Her Majesty Queen Elizabeth II and the date of her 90th birthday - 21st April 2016. [...]

Year of Issue: 2016
Diameter: 38.61 mm
Denomination: £5

1. fait figurer – 2. représente

CONSEILS

Lis le texte avec attention. Tu peux faire une liste de tous les éléments présents sur la pièce. Concentre-toi sur le vocabulaire.

3 New British coin

1. Match the words from the text to their synonyms.

sovereign	famous
celebrate	monogram
issued	put in circulation
momentous	present
brand-new	queen
feature	commemorate
renowned	historic
depict	absolutely new
cypher	reproduce

2. Read and comment on the text. Choose between the following exercises (A or B).

ACCOMPAGNEMENT PERSONNALISÉ AP

DIFFÉRENCIATION

A

First reading

a. What is the text about?
It is about...
- [ ] a new £10 coin.
- [x] a new £5 coin.
- [ ] a new £2 coin.

b. Why was it issued?
It was issued...
- [ ] to celebrate Queen Elizabeth II's jubilee.
- [ ] to celebrate Queen Elizabeth I's birthday.
- [x] to celebrate Queen Elizabeth II's 90th birthday.

c. What material is it made of?
It is made of...
- [x] gold.
- [ ] silver.
- [ ] brass.

Second reading

d. Speak about the obverse.
What can you see ?
I can see...
- [ ] a portrait of young Queen Elizabeth II.
- [ ] a portrait of the Queen mother.
- [x] a portrait of Queen Elizabeth aged ninety.

e. Who designed the portrait?
- [ ] Michael Guilfoyle.
- [ ] Christopher Wren.
- [x] Luigi Badia.

Third reading

f. Speak about the reverse.
What can you see?
I can see...
- [ ] the Union Jack and the Royal flag, 90, the royal monogram (EII R) and April 21st 2016.
- [x] the Union Jack and the Royal flag, 90, the royal monogram (EII R), the words Her Majesty Queen Elizabeth II and April 21st 2016.

g. What does April 21st 2016 correspond to? It corresponds to...
- [ ] the Queen's date of birth.
- [ ] the beginning of her reign.
- [x] the day of her 90th birthday.

B

First reading

a. What is the text about?

The text is about a new £5 coin / a new Queen Elizabeth II coin.

b. Why was it issued?

It was issued to celebrate the Queen's 90th birthday.

c. What material is it made of?

It is made of gold.

Second reading

d. Speak about the obverse. What can you see?

I can see a portrait of Queen Elizabeth II.

e. Who designed the portrait?

Luigi Badia designed the portrait.

Third reading

f. Speak about the reverse. What can you see?

I can see the union and royal standard flags with 90 at the center and the royal cypher above, encircled by the words Her Majesty Queen Elizabeth II and the date of her 90th birthday.

g. What does April 21st 2016 correspond to?

It corresponds to the Queen's 90th birthday.

CONSEILS

Aide-toi de l'exercice 1 pour mieux comprendre le texte. Il te permettra de répondre aux questions plus facilement.
Tu peux utiliser le vocabulaire vu dans le manuel et dans les leçons précédentes. Sois attentif aux questions.

Vocabulary

- £1≈ 1,11 €
- £5 ≈ 5,55 €

4 The Queen's house

GET READY!

→ Book p. 91

Look at the documents and answer the questions.

Queen Elizabeth II in the White Drawing Room

Queen Elizabeth II sits in the Regency Room

1. Who can you see on the photos?

a. On the first photo, I can see... ☐ Queen Elizabeth and her family. ☑ Queen Elizabeth and three men.

b. Where is she in the first picture?
She is... ☐ in the Drawing Room. ☑ in the White Drawing Room. ☐ in the Gold Drawing Room.

c. What room do you think it is? It is... ☐ a kitchen. ☐ a bedroom. ☑ a living-room.

d. Where is the Queen in the second picture?
She is... ☑ in the Regency Room. ☐ in the Regent Room. ☐ in the Queen's Room.

e. This is... ☐ her bedroom. ☐ her bathroom. ☑ her office.

2. Talk about the furniture.

a. What decorations are there in the first picture?
There are...
☑ a huge painting, an immense portrait of the Queen, many chandeliers and a large carpeted floor.
☐ a small portrait of the Queen and candelabra.

b. In the second picture there are... ☐ a piano, a desk, many chairs and a sofa.
☑ a sofa, an armchair, two writing-desks.
☐ armchairs, a sofa, a table and a bed.

c. What do these rooms look like?
They look... ☐ very simple. ☑ very luxurious. ☐ extremely modern.

GO! → Book p. 91

Read the text and do the following exercises.

CONSEILS

Tu vas lire le texte plusieurs fois. Concentre-toi sur les noms de lieux. Fais une liste des noms propres pour t'aider.

Where Does the Queen Live?

Buckingham Palace is the Queen's office[1] as well as her London home. The part most tourists see is the East Front. Here is the balcony where the royal family appears sometimes. The gardens are used for summer garden parties.

The Queen has a country house at Sandringham in Norfolk. In Scotland, her official residence is Holyroodhouse, in Edinburgh. In summer the Queen holidays in Scotland, at Balmoral Castle in Aberdeenshire. While she is away, the state rooms at Buckingham Palace are open to visitors.

Windsor Castle in Berkshire is a favourite royal home. It is the oldest and biggest castle still used as a home. Windsor Castle was begun in 1070 by William the Conqueror.

In 1992 fire burned[2] down parts of Windsor Castle. The Queen was sad, and helped to pay for repairs that have made the castle as splendid as ever.

www.bbc.co.uk

1. bureau – 2. brûla

1. Pick up in the text all the words refering to a place, a city or a country.
Help: Look at the capital letters!

Buckingham Palace / London / Sandringham / Norfolk / Scotland / Holyroodhouse /

Edinburgh / Balmoral Castle / Aberdeenshire / Windsor Castle / Berkshire.

2. Read and comment on the text. Choose between the following exercises (A or B).

A

AP ACCOMPAGNEMENT PERSONNALISÉ
DIFFÉRENCIATION

First reading

a. What is the text about?
The text is about... ☐ the British Royal family.
☑ the different residences of the Queen.
☐ Buckingham Palace.

b. Where does the Queen live in London?
She lives... ☐ at 10 Downing Street. ☑ at Buckingham Palace. ☐ at Sandringham.

c. It is also... ☑ her office. ☐ her place of birth. ☐ her favourite home.

d. Which part of the palace do the tourists see?
They see... ☐ the West front. ☑ the East front. ☐ the North front.

e. The Royal family sometimes... ☐ has breakfast. ☐ sleeps. ☑ appears on the balcony.

4 The Queen's house

Second reading

f. How many "houses" does the Queen have? ☑ 5 ☐ 3 ☐ 4

g. They are:

☐ Buckingham Palace, Holyroodhouse and Windsor Castle.

☐ Buckingham Palace, a house in Sandringham, Holyroodhouse and Windsor Castle.

☑ Buckingham Palace, a house in Sandringham, Holyroodhouse, Balmoral Castle and Windsor Castle.

h. Which house is her main residence?

It is... ☐ Holyroodhouse. ☑ Buckingham Palace. ☐ Windsor Castle.

i. When she is not there, what can tourists do? They can...

☐ have a garden party in the gardens. ☑ visit the state rooms of the palace. ☐ sleep at the palace.

Third reading

j. What happened in 1992?

☑ Fire destroyed parts of Windsor Castle.

☐ Fire completely destroyed Windsor Castle.

☐ Fire destroyed Balmoral Castle.

k. The Queen was very sad because it is her... ☐ main castle. ☑ favourite castle. ☐ safest castle.

l. The castle is very old, it dates back to... ☐ 1066. ☐ 1077. ☑ 1070.

m. Who built the castle? ☑ William The Conqueror. ☐ Sir Christopher Wren. ☐ Gustave Eiffel.

n. What did the Queen do? ☐ She built a new castle. ☑ She helped to pay for repairs. ☐ She moved away.

B

First reading

a. What is the text about?

The text is about the residences/houses of the Queen.

b. Where does the Queen live in London?

She lives at Buckingham Palace. It is also her office.

c. Which part of the palace do the tourists see?

They see the East front.

d. The Royal family sometimes appears on the balcony.

Second reading

e. How many "houses" does the Queen have? She has five residences.

f. They are: Buckingham Palace, a house in Sandringham, Holyroodhouse, Balmoral Castle and Windsor Castle.

g. Which house is her main residence? It is Buckingham Palace.

h. When she is not there, what can tourists do?

They can visit the state rooms of the palace.

Third reading

i. What happened in 1992? A fire burned down parts of Windsor Castle.

j. Why was the Queen very sad? The Queen was very sad because it is her favourite castle.

k. Is the castle very old? Yes, the castle is very old, it dates back to 1070.

l. Who built it? William the Conqueror built the castle.

m. What did the Queen do? She helped to pay for repairs.

PREPARE YOUR FINAL TASKS

→ Book p. 91

Talk about the Queen's everyday life.

Explain where the Queen lives and works every day and where she goes on holidays.

The Queen lives and works at... It is in... When she does not work, she can go to...

CONSEILS

- Aide-toi de ce que tu sais déjà sur la reine.
- Sers-toi des exercices précédents n'oublie pas ta liste de noms propres, elle peut t'aider !

Vocabulary

- **fur**niture
- candel**a**bra
- main
- **mo**ved away

5 The line of succession

GET READY! → Book p. 92

Look at the document and answer the questions.

1. What is the document about?

- ☐ The marriage of a Royal family's member.
- ☑ Queen Elizabeth II's line of succession.
- ☑ The birth of a new baby in the Royal family.
- ☐ Queen Elizabeth II's date of birth.

2. Who can you see on the document?

a. I can see... ☐ Queen Elizabeth's children. ☑ Queen Elizabeth's direct heirs. ☐ Queen Elizabeth's parents.

b. Who is Queen Elizabeth's first heir in the line of succession?

☑ Prince Charles ☐ Prince William ☐ Prince Harry ☐ Prince George

c. Who is Queen Elizabeth's second heir in the line of succession?

☐ Prince George ☐ Princess Charlotte ☑ Prince William

GO! → Book p. 92

Read and comment on the text.

CONSEILS
- Lis le texte. Avec l'aide de l'arbre
- généalogique, tu vas pouvoir répondre
- aux questions. Sois très attentif.

The Duke and Duchess said congratulations they have received from the public meant "a great deal". They were "hugely grateful" for the kind wishes[1] of people celebrating their newborn daughter's birth. Carole, Pippa and Michael Middleton visited the baby this afternoon alongside Prince Charles and Camilla. The Queen is in Sandringham and will likely meet her great-grandchild there. The princess, whose name is Charlotte, was born on May 2nd 2015 at the Lindo Wing of St Mary's Hospital weighing 8 lbs and 3 oz[2].

Adapted from: www.dailymail.co.uk

1. vœux de bonheur – 2. 8 lbs and 3 oz : 3,71 kg

Choose between the following exercises (A or B).

AP ACCOMPAGNEMENT PERSONNALISÉ

DIFFÉRENCIATION

A

First reading

a. Read the text. It is...
- ☐ an extract from a book. ☐ a magazine article. ☑ a newspaper article in the Daily Mail.

b. What is the text about?
- ☐ Kate and William's son. ☑ Princess Charlotte's birth. ☐ Kate and William's wedding.

c. When was Charlotte born? ☐ On May 2nd 2014. ☑ On May 2nd 2015. ☐ On May 2nd 2016.

Second reading

d. How did Kate and William feel after Charlotte's birth?

They were very happy because...
- ☐ they received lots of presents.
- ☑ they received lots of congratulations.
- ☑ they received kind wishes.

e. Say what you understand: "it meant a great deal" and "they were hugely grateful" means...
- ☑ it was really important to them and they were very pleased.
- ☐ they were not pleased to receive kind wishes.
- ☐ they were very surprised.

Third reading

f. Write about Charlotte and her family. What was Charlotte's weight when she was born?
☐ 6 lbs 3 oz. ☑ 8 lbs and 3 oz. ☐ 8 lbs 2 oz.

g. Where was she born? ☐ At home. ☑ In a hospital. ☐ At Kensington Palace.

h. Who visited the baby? ☑ Her grandparents. ☐ Her great-grandmother Queen Elizabeth.

i. Is Charlotte Kate and William's first baby? ☐ Yes, she is. ☑ No, she has a brother named George.

B

First reading

a. What sort of text is it and what is it about? The text is a newspaper article in the Daily Mail about Princess Charlotte's birth.

b. When was Charlotte born? She was born on May 2nd 2015.

Second reading

d. What were Kate and William's feelings after Charlotte's birth?

They were very happy because they received lots of congratulations and they received kind wishes.

e. Say what you understand:
"it meant a great deal" and "they were hugely grateful" means...

It was really important to them and they were very pleased.

Third reading

Write about Charlotte and her family.

g. Who is Princess Charlotte's brother? Prince George is Charlotte's brother.

h. What was her weight when she was born? She weighed 8 lbs and 3 oz.

i. Where was she born? She was born in St Mary's Hospital.

CONSEILS

- Tu peux t'aider en écrivant tous les noms propres du texte sur ton cahier. Pour déterminer les liens de parenté, pars des personnes que tu connais déjà.

Vocabulary

- heir
- a great deal
- congratu**la**tions
- weight
- **hu**gely **gra**teful
- kind
- **li**kely

6 Jubilee street party

GET READY!

→ Book p. 93

Look at the document and answer the questions.

Queen's Diamond Jubilee Celebrations, street party, London, Britain, June 4th 2012

1. Say what you can see.

a. Where are the people?

- ☐ At a concert. ☑ In the street. ☐ In a restaurant.

b. What are they holding?

- ☐ American flags. ☑ Bags with the Union Jack on them.
- ☐ English flags.

2. Say what the people are doing and why.

a. They are...

- ☐ dancing.
- ☑ having a street party.
- ☑ celebrating an important event.

b. What are they celebrating?

- ☐ The Queen's birthday.
- ☑ The Queen's Diamond Jubilee.
- ☐ The Queen's coronation.

GO!

VIDEO 16

→ Book p. 93

Comment on the video. Choose between the following exercises (A or B).

ACCOMPAGNEMENT PERSONNALISÉ AP

DIFFÉRENCIATION

CONSEILS

Regarde la vidéo. Sois attentif au discours mais aussi à ce qui se passe sur la scène. Repère les personnes présentes.

A

First viewing

a. What sort of event was it?

- ☑ A concert. ☐ A political meeting. ☐ A festival.

b. What was the event for?

- ☐ Queen Elizabeth II's birthday. ☑ Queen Elizabeth II's Diamond Jubilee.

c. What other members of the Royal family can you see?

- ☑ Camilla. ☐ Katherine Middleton. ☑ Charles. ☑ William. ☑ Harry. ☐ Prince Philip.

d. Who made the speech? ....Prince Charles........ made the speech.

Second viewing

e. What did Prince Charles talk about?

- ☐ His father's life and reign. ☑ His mother's life and reign.

f. How did he call his mother?

- ☐ "her Royal Highness". ☑ "her Majesty". ☑ "mummy".

g. Talk about her reaction.
She looks... ☑ pleased. ☐ angry. ☑ moved.

Third viewing

h. Say what you understand about the Jubilee.
The Diamond Jubilee was...
☐ a rare and boring event. ☑ a unique and special event. ☐ a sad and special event.

i. They already celebrated:
☐ 2 Jubilees. ☑ 3 Jubilees. ☐ 4 Jubilees.

j. What did they celebrate at the Diamond Jubilee?
☑ 60 years of life and services of Queen Elizabeth II.
☐ The life and death of Queen Elizabeth II.
☐ 50 years of life and services of Prince Charles.

CONSEILS
Regarde à nouveau la vidéo. Note les mots que tu ne comprends pas. Concentre-toi d'abord sur Charles, puis sur ce qui se passe sur scène.

B

First viewing

a. What sort of event was it? It was a concert.

b. What singers do you recognize?

I recognize Paul Mc Cartney, Elton John, Kylie Minogue...

c. What was the event for?

The event was for Queen Elizabeth II's Diamond Jubilee.

d. What other members of the Royal family can you see?

I can see Camilla, Charles, William and Harry.

e. Who made the speech?

Charles made the speech. He is the Queen's first son.

Second viewing

f. What did Charles talk about?

He talked about his mother's life and reign.

g. How did he call her?

He called her "her Majesty" and "mummy".

CONSEILS

Regarde la page *Find out more* du manuel et découvre les paroles de l'hymne national britannique.

h. Talk about her reaction. How did she look?

She looked pleased and moved.

Third viewing

i. Say what you understand about the Jubilee. What was the Diamond Jubilee?

It was a unique and special event.

j. How many Jubilees did they celebrate before?

They celebrated 3 Jubilees before.

k. What did they celebrate at the Diamond Jubilee?

They celebrated the life and services of Queen Elizabeth II.

l. What did the Diamond Jubilee correspond to?

It corresponds to 60 years of services and duty.

PREPARE YOUR FINAL TASKS

→ Book p. 93

Write a few sentences to explain what the Diamond Jubilee was about.

The Jubilee was about... People wanted to celebrate... They loved...

CONSEILS

Sers-toi du texte et des questions des grilles pour t'aider à rédiger tes phrases.
Regarde à nouveau la vidéo. Le discours du Prince Charles peut t'aider. Regarde aussi l'image de la page 123.

Vocabulary

- band
- joke
- clap **hands**
- duty
- moved
- dedi**ca**tion
- **ce**lebrate
- **re**cognize

Language practice GRAMMAR

L'expression de la durée → Book p. 95

Pour indiquer le temps qui s'est écoulé depuis un événement, j'utilise ......ago...... précédé du temps écoulé.

– Twenty years ......ago...... .

– Six weeks ......ago...... .

Pour indiquer la durée d'une action, j'utilise ......for...... suivi du temps écoulé :

– ......For...... 10 years.

– ......For...... 6 months.

1 Remets les mots dans le bon ordre.

a. 35 / Henry I / reigned / years / for

Henry I reigned for 35 years.

b. not / for / reign / did / Henry VI / years / 40

Henry VI did not reign for 40 years.

c. for / was / Queen Victoria / British / 63 / the / years / monarch

Queen Victoria was the British monarch for 63 years.

d. throne / the / years / Elizabeth I / on / for / sat / 44

Elizabeth I sat on the throne for 44 years.

e. years / was / king / British / 56 / for / the / Henry IV

Henry IV was the British king for 56 years.

2 Utilise *ago* pour compléter les phrases suivantes. L'année actuelle doit être ton repère !

a. Queen Elizabeth II was born (1926) .... years ago.

b. She became Queen (1952) .... ago.

c. Queen Victoria became Queen (1837) .... ago.

d. And she died (1901) .... ago.

e. She celebrated her 80th birthday (21/04/2006) .... ago.

Le prétérit régulier et irrégulier → Book p. 95

Pour écrire une biographie j'utilise ......le prétérit......

Pour les verbes réguliers, j'ajoute ......-ed...... à la ......BV.......

Les verbes irréguliers s'apprennent ......par cœur...... !

3 À l'aide des dates, rédige une courte biographie du prince Charles, le fils aîné d'Elizabeth II.

1948: Birth of Prince Charles.
1967: Job: pilot.
1981: First wedding: Diana Spencer ("Lady Di").
1982: First son, William.
1984: Second son, Harry.
1996: Divorce.
2005: Second wedding: Camilla Parker Bowles.
2013: Grandfather: Prince George's birth.
2015: Grandfather for the second time: Princess Charlotte's birth.

L'article *the* ou ø → Book p. 95

Lorsque je désigne un membre de la famille royale par son titre seul, j'utilise le déterminant ......the...... :

......The...... Queen of England.

Lorsque je désigne un membre de la famille royale (son titre, sa fonction suivi de son nom), je n'utilise pas de déterminant :

...ø... Queen Elizabeth II.

4 Complète les phrases suivantes par *the* lorsque cela est nécessaire.

a. ...ø... Prince Charles is ......ø...... Queen Elizabeth's eldest son.

b. ......The...... Duchess of Cambridge is Kate Middleton.

c. ......ø...... Prince William is also ......the...... Duke of Cambridge.

d. ......The...... Queen of England is married to ......ø...... Prince Phillip.

e. ......ø...... Prince George is ......the...... future King of England!

Whose et le cas possessif → Book p. 96

• Pour poser une question sur un lien de parenté j'utilise « ......whose...... » :

......Whose...... daughter is Charlotte?

• Le génitif, symbolisé par ......'s...... sert à marquer un lien de ......parenté.......

George is William and Kate ......'s...... son.

5 Trouve la personne dont il s'agit.

a. He is Charlotte's grandfather. Prince Charles

b. She is William's wife. Catherine, Duchess of Cambridge

c. He is Charlotte and George's uncle. Harry, Prince of Wales.

Language practice PHONOLOGY

Le son [ə] des mots qui se terminent par *-er* ou *-or*. → Book p. 96

Les mots terminés par -er ou -or se prononcent toujours de la même façon c'est-à-dire [ə].

1 Classe les mots suivants dans le tableau.

gardener / conquer / summer / winter / ornament

[ə]		Autre son
gardener	summer	ornament
conquer	winter	

Le son [eɪ] et le son [æ] → Book p. 96

Le son [eɪ] est un son long et le son [æ] est un son bref.

2 Classe les mots suivants dans le tableau.

celebration / weigh / had / baby / name

[eɪ]	[æ]
celebration	grandson
weigh	had
baby	
name	

Auto-évaluation

➔ Book p. 100

Connaissances et compétences linguistiques

Vocabulary

- Je connais le vocabulaire se rapportant à la monarchie.
- Je connais le vocabulaire de la monnaie anglaise.

Grammar

- Je sais utiliser le prétérit simple régulier et irrégulier.
- Je sais exprimer la durée avec *ago* et *for*.
- Je sais utiliser le prétérit simple régulier et irrégulier.
- Je sais utiliser l'article *the* et Ø.
- Je sais utiliser *whose* et le génitif pour parler des liens de parenté et d'appartenance.

Phonology

- Le son [ə] des mots qui se terminent par *-er* ou *-or*.
- Je sais distinguer les sons [eɪ] et [æ].

Compétences langagières et domaines du socle commun

Écouter et comprendre
Domaines 1, 2
- Je sais comprendre une vidéo.

Lire et comprendre
Domaines 1, 2
- Je sais lire et comprendre les points essentiels d'un texte ou article.
- Je sais repérer les informations essentielles d'un document extrait d'un site Internet.

Parler en continu
Domaines 1, 2, 3
- Je sais raconter ce qui se passe dans une vidéo.

Écrire
Domaines 1, 2, 5
- Je sais écrire un texte court au passé.
- Je sais écrire une biographie.

Réagir et dialoguer
Domaines 1, 2
- Je sais faire des commentaires sur les différents aspects de la vie de la reine.

PEAC

Culture et Parcours
Domaines 1, 2, 3, 5
- Je connais la biographie de la reine Elizabeth II et les grands événements qui ont ponctué son règne.
- Je connais les principaux membres de la famille royale.

7 American music

1 The King and Memphis

GET READY! → Book p. 102 30 CD2

1. Talk about Elvis Presley.

a. When was he born?

- [x] On January 8th 1935.
- [ ] On January 8th 1925.
- [ ] On June 8th 1935.

b. Where was he born?

- [ ] In Tupelo, Missouri.
- [ ] In Tubelo, Mississippi.
- [x] In Tupelo, Mississippi.

2. What styles of music was he influenced by?

- [ ] Jazz music.
- [ ] Rap music.
- [ ] Classical music.
- [x] RnB music.
- [x] Country music.
- [x] Gospel.

3. How did he become famous?

a. What happened in 1953?

- [ ] He was discovered by a manager.
- [x] He walked into a song studio.
- [x] He recorded a two-song demo.
- [ ] He recorded an album.

b. How much did he pay to record it?

- [ ] 3 dollars.
- [x] 4 dollars.
- [ ] 40 dollars.

c. What song became a hit?

- [ ] Jailhouse Rock.
- [x] That's all right.
- [ ] Blue Suede shoes.

GO! → Book p. 102 VIDEO 17

Watch and react. Choose between the following exercises (A or B).

ACCOMPAGNEMENT PERSONNALISÉ AP

DIFFÉRENCIATION

Well it's one for the money, two for the show
Three to get ready, now go cat go
But don't you, step on my blue suede shoes
You can do anything but lay off of my blue suede shoes
But you can knock me down, step in my face
Slander my name all over the place
And do anything that you want to do
But uh uh honey lay off of my shoes
And don't you step on my blue suede shoes
You can do anything but lay off of my blue suede shoes.

CONSEILS

Tu vas écouter un extrait de la chanson Blue Suede Shoes d'Elvis Presley et lire un extrait des paroles. Sois attentif à la construction des phrases, aux mots qui sont répétés, etc. Note tous les termes que tu ne comprends pas.

A

First viewing

a. What is he talking about?

☐ His blue boots. ☑ His blue suede shoes. ☐ His blue leather shoes.

b. What does he keep repeating? Write the sentences.

But don't you, step on my blue suede shoes. You can do anything but lay off of my blue suede shoes.

c. How often do the words "blues suede shoes" come back in the text?

☐ Once. ☑ 4 times. ☐ More than 4 times.

d. Can you pick up any rhymes in the song? Circle the words you hear:

shout / (show) / blow / (go) / (do) / (shoes) / race / (place) / (face)

Second viewing

e. What style of music is it?

☑ Rock'n roll music.
☐ Pop music.
☐ Jazz music.

f. Talk about the rhythm.
It is very...

☐ slow.
☑ fast.
☑ dynamic.

g. There are also elements of...

☑ blues.
☑ country music.
☐ classical music.

h. How do you feel when you listen to the song?

☑ Happy.
☐ Sad.
☑ You feel like dancing.
☐ You feel depressed.

Third viewing

i. Talk about the rhyme. Most words have only...

☑ 1 syllable. ☐ 2 syllables. ☐ 3 syllables.

j. Listen again: "it's one for the money, two for the show, three to get ready". What impression do counting and short words give? It makes the song very...

☐ moderate. ☑ rhythmic. ☑ energetic. ☐ calm.

k. His shoes are blue and made of suede (*daim*), so they are very...

☑ original. ☐ neutral.

l. "but don't you step on my blue suede shoes", "you can do anything but lay off of my shoes". What is the message of this song?

☐ People must respect his shoes because they are expensive and new.
☑ People must respect the way he looks, even if it is different.
☑ They must accept the way he dresses, even if it is original.

m. Do you know how rock'n' roll music was considered in those days?

☑ Rebellious and revolutionary.
☐ Modest and safe.

B

First viewing

a. What is he talking about?

He is talking about his blue suede shoes.

b. What does he keep repeating? Write the sentences.

"But don't you step on my blue suede shoes

You can do anything but lay off of my blue suede shoes."

c. Can you pick up any rhymes in the song? Concentrate on the accentuated words.

show / go / do / shoes / place / face

Second viewing

d. What style of music is it?

It is rock'n roll music.

e. Talk about the rhythm. How would you describe it?

It is very dynamic.

f. There are also elements of...

- [x] blues
- [x] country music
- [ ] classical music

g. How do you feel when you listen to the song?

I want to dance.

I feel like dancing.

I feel energetic.

Third viewing

h. Talk about the rhyme. How many syllables do most words have?

Most words have one syllable.

i. Listen again: "it's one for the money, two for the show, three to get ready". What impression do counting and short words give? Find adjectives to describe it.

It makes the song very rhythmic and energetic.

j. His shoes are blue and made of suede (*daim*), so they are very...

- [x] original.
- [ ] neutral.

k. "but don't you step on my blue suede shoes", "you can do anything but lay off of my shoes". What is the message of this song?

- [ ] People must respect his shoes because they are expensive and new.
- [x] People must respect the way he looks, even if it is different.
- [x] People must accept the way he dresses, even if it is original.

l. Do you know how rock'n' roll music was considered in those days?
Choose adjectives in the list below which could describe it.

safe / dangerous / respectful / rebellious / law-abiding / subversive / revolutionary / inoffensive.

CONSEILS

- Écoute bien la chanson.
- Imprègne-toi de la musique et du rythme.
- Essaie de repérer le refrain et répète-le à haute voix.

Vocabulary

- **slan**der: *diffamer*
- **step** on = walk on
- lay off = don't touch
- knock someone **down** = hit someone hard so that the person falls

2 Prince and Minneapolis

GET READY!

→ Book p. 103 33 CD2

1. Who is this man?

a. He is...

- [ ] an actor.
- [ ] a dancer.
- [x] a singer.
- [x] a musician.

b. What's his name?
His name is...

- [x] Prince
- [ ] The Prince
- [ ] The King

2. What do you know about him?

a. He is...

- [ ] English.
- [ ] Australian.
- [x] American.

b. He is...

- [ ] alive.
- [x] dead.

c. He looked...

- [x] quite eccentric.
- [ ] very classical.

d. He played...

- [ ] the saxophone.
- [x] the electric guitar.
- [ ] the drums.

CONSEILS

- Écoute la chanson.
- Lis les paroles ci-dessous en même temps et
- concentre-toi sur la musique.

GO!

→ Book p. 103

1. Match the words to their synonyms.

the lyrics •	• a regular series of sounds or movements.
the rhythm •	• a part of a song which is repeated after each verse.
the chorus •	• the words of a song.
a verse •	• one of the parts of a song.

(Lines drawn: the lyrics → the words of a song; the rhythm → a regular series of sounds or movements; the chorus → a part of a song which is repeated after each verse; a verse → one of the parts of a song.)

2. Now complete the sentences with the correct words.

From line 1 to 5

it is the verse.

From line 6 to 10

it is the chorus.

From line 1 to 10

they are the lyrics.

I never meant to cause you any sorrow
I never meant to cause you any pain
I only wanted to one time to see you laughing
I only wanted to see you
Laughing in the purple rain
Purple rain, purple rain
Purple rain, purple rain
Purple rain, purple rain
I only wanted to see you
Bathing in the purple rain...

AP ACCOMPAGNEMENT PERSONNALISÉ

DIFFÉRENCIATION

3. **Comment on the audio. Choose between the following exercises (A or B).**

A

First listening

a. The rhythm is very...
- [x] slow.
- [ ] fast.

b. What type of song is it?
It is...
- [ ] rock'n'roll music.
- [ ] pop music.
- [x] a ballad.

Second listening

c. What are the singer's feelings?
He sounds...
- [ ] very happy and enthusiastic.
- [x] quite sad.
- [ ] totally indifferent.

d. Tick the two words that best reflect his feelings:
- [x] sorrow
- [ ] rain
- [x] pain
- [ ] bathing
- [ ] laughing

e. They are synonymous of...
- [ ] happiness.
- [x] sadness.
- [ ] pleasure.
- [x] suffering.

Third listening

f. What is the singer's message?
He speaks to someone he...
- [x] loves.
- [ ] hates.

g. He wants...
- [x] to apologize/say sorry.
- [ ] to make fun of this person.

h. He wants this person...
- [ ] to feel sad.
- [x] to feel happy.

B

First listening

What type of song is it?

a. The rhythm is very ....slow........ .

b. The song is... ....a ballad, a slow dance........ .

Second listening

c. What are the singer's feelings? He sounds ....sad, disappointed........ .

d. Find in the lyrics the two words that best reflect his feelings.

The two words are ....sorrow........ and ....pain........ .

e. They are synonymous of...
- [ ] happiness.
- [x] sadness.
- [ ] pleasure.
- [x] suffering.

Third listening

f. What is the singer's message?
He speaks to someone he ....loves........ .

CONSEILS

Écoute attentivement la chanson de Prince. Pour t'aider, souviens-toi de la chanson d'Elvis. Note les mots qui reviennent régulièrement.

Vocabulary

- release

g. He wants...

- [x] to apologize/say sorry.
- [ ] to make fun of this person.

h. He wants this person...

to feel happy.

PREPARE YOUR FINAL TASKS → Book p. 103

Select the most important moments in Prince's musical career and write a short paragraph.

CONSEILS

N'écris pas un paragraphe trop long. Contente toi des moments les plus marquants de sa carrière.

3 Hip Hop in New York

GET READY! → Book p. 104

Look at the pictures and answer the questions.

1. What can you say about the people in the pictures?

- [x] I think they are musicians and singers.
- [ ] I think they are fashion models.

2. What is their music style?

- [ ] Jazz music.
- [x] Hip Hop music.
- [ ] Country music.

A Tribe Called Quest

Wu-Tang Clan

2PAC

Public Enemy

NAS

3 Hip Hop in New York

GO! VIDEO 18 → Book p. 104

ACCOMPAGNEMENT PERSONNALISÉ AP

Comment on the video. Choose between the following exercises (A or B). DIFFÉRENCIATION

A

CONSEILS

- Regarde la vidéo trois fois.
- Essaie d'abord de repérer le sens global en t'aidant des images.
- Ensuite, concentre-toi sur les mots que tu connais pour t'aider à comprendre.

First viewing

a. Who can you see in the video?

☑ Rappers. ☐ Actors. ☐ Dancers.

b. Why are the songs in this video special?

☐ They are the top 10 important albums in rock'n'roll history.
☑ They are the top 10 important albums in Hip Hop history.
☐ They are the top 10 important albums in classical music.

c. What is the period these albums cover?

☐ 1960-1980. ☑ 1980-2000. ☐ 2000-2020.

Second viewing

d. List all the artists and their songs. Listen to the songs and complete their titles.

1. *Method Man*
2. *The World Is Yours*
3. *Let Me Ride*
4. *Big Poppa*
5. *Straight Outta Compton*
6. *Don't Believe the Hype*
7. *The Way I Am*
8. *So Many Tears*
9. *Sucker MCs'*
10. *I Ain't No Joke*

e. Write the artist's names in front of the corresponding albums.

– *Me Against the World:* 2PAC (1994)

– *Ready to Die:* The Notorious B.I.G. (1994)

– *The Marshall Mathers LP:* Eminem (2000)

– *The Chronic:* Dr. Dre (1992)

Third viewing

f. Describe what Hip Hop music is associated with. What do you notice about the rappers in the video?

☑ They are all black males. ☐ They are all black females.

g. There is an exception. Who is it?

☑ Eminem. ☐ Elvis Presley. ☐ Michael Jackson.

h. What clothes and accessories do they wear?

☐ Suits. ☑ Tracksuits. ☐ Ties. ☑ Baggy trousers. ☐ Slim pants. ☑ Flashy jewels.

i. Describe Hip Hop music's rhythm.

☐ Weak beats. ☑ Quick. ☑ Strong beats. ☐ Quiet. ☐ Delicate. ☑ Cadenced.

B

First viewing

a. Who can you see in the video? I can see rappers.

b. Why are the songs in this video special?

They are the top 10 important albums in Hip Hop history.

c. What is the period these albums cover?

They cover the period from 1980 to 2000.

Second viewing

d. List all the artists and their songs.

1. *Method Man*
2. *The World Is Yours*
3. *Let Me Ride*
4. *Big Poppa*
5. *Straight Outta Compton*
6. *Don't Believe the Hype*
7. *The Way I Am*
8. *So Many Tears*
9. *Sucker MCs'*
10. *I Ain't No Joke*

e. Write the artists' names in front of the corresponding albums.

– *Me Against the World:* 2PAC (1994)

– *Ready to Die:* The Notorious B.I.G. (1994)

– *The Marshall Mathers LP:* Eminem (2000)

– *The Chronic:* Dr. Dre (1992)

Third viewing

f. What do you notice about the rappers in the video?

☑ They are all black males. ☐ They are all black females.

g. There is an exception. Who is it?

Eminem is the exception.

h. What clothes and accessories do they wear?

They wear tracksuits, baggy trousers and flashy jewels.

i. Describe Hip Hop music's rhythm.

☐ Weak beats. ☐ Quiet. ☑ Quick.

☐ Delicate. ☑ Strong beats. ☑ Cadenced.

CONSEILS

Aide toi des titres des chansons dans la vidéo pour compléter ta grille d'écoute. Regarde attentivement les extraits pour répondre aux questions. Sois attentif aux détails : façon de chanter, de s'habiller, rythme et paroles...

Vocabulary

- **male** = man
- **female** = woman
- **pants** = trousers
- **jewels** = necklace, ring, bracelet...
- **beat** = cadence/ rhythm

4 The Jackson Five and Motown

GET READY! ➔ Book p. 105

Look and react.

1. What do you know about the Jackson Five?

a. They were... [ ] friends. [ ] neighbours. [x] brothers.

b. They were... [ ] dancers. [x] singers. [ ] actors.

c. Jackson was... [x] their family name. [ ] their stage name.

d. They were... [ ] quite famous. [x] very famous. [ ] not famous at all.

e. Which member of the Jackson Five became the most famous one?

Michael Jackson became the most famous one.

2. When do you think the photo was taken?

a. I think the photo was taken in...

[ ] the 50s (the fifties).
[ ] the 60s (the sixties).
[x] the 70s (the seventies).

b. I chose this period because of...

[x] their hairstyle.
[ ] their music instruments.
[x] their flashy clothes.

c. In those years, they sang...

[ ] Hip Hop music.
[x] pop and soul music.
[ ] traditional American music.

GO! VIDEO → Book p. 105

Watch and comment on the video. Choose between the following exercises (A or B).

AP ACCOMPAGNEMENT PERSONNALISÉ

DIFFÉRENCIATION

CONSEILS

Regarde plusieurs fois la vidéo. Sois attentif aux paroles, au groupe, au rythme. Souviens-toi de ce que tu as vu aux leçons précédentes sur les chansons de Prince et d'Elvis.

A

First viewing

a. Talk about the song.
What was the title of the song?
- [ ] "I want your back"
- [x] "I want you back"
- [ ] "I want her back"

b. What sort of song was it?
It was a...
- [ ] rhythm and blues song.
- [x] pop song.
- [ ] rock'n'roll song.

c. This style of music...
- [x] has a good rhythm.
- [ ] has a slow rhythm.
- [x] is easy to remember.
- [ ] is difficult to remember.

Second viewing

Give information about the five brothers.

d. How many brothers had an instrument?
- [x] Two of them.
- [ ] Three of them.
- [ ] Five of them.

e. What instruments did they have?
They had...
- [ ] flutes.
- [ ] drums.
- [x] electric guitars.

f. What were all the brothers doing?
They were...
- [ ] smiling.
- [ ] dancing.
- [x] singing and dancing.

Third viewing

Give information about Michael.

g. Who was Michael compared to his brothers?
Michael was...
- [ ] the eldest.
- [x] the youngest.

h. What sort of costume was he wearing?
He was wearing...
- [x] a flashy costume.
- [ ] a dark costume.
- [ ] a pink costume.

i. He was...
- [x] the first one to sing.
- [ ] the second one to sing.
- [ ] the last one to sing.

j. What part did he play in the band? He was...
- [x] the lead singer.
- [ ] part of the choir.
- [ ] a dancer.

B

First viewing

a. Talk about the song. What was the title of the song?

It was "I want you back".

b. What sort of song was it?

It was a pop song.

4 The Jackson Five and Motown

Second viewing

Give information about the five brothers.

c. How many brothers had an instrument?

Two brothers had an instrument.

d. What instruments did they have?

They had electric guitars.

e. What were all the brothers doing?

They were singing and dancing.

Third viewing

Give information about Michael.

f. Who was Michael compared to his brothers?

Michael was the youngest brother of the Jackson Five.

g. What sort of costume was he wearing?

He was wearing a flashy costume.

h. What part did he play in the band? Complete with the appropriate word: best, lead, worst, last.

He was the lead singer.

CONSEILS

Il n'est pas nécessaire de comprendre toutes les paroles de la chanson pour remplir la grille. Sois plutôt observateur !

Vocabulary

- drums = percussion instrument
- lead **sin**ger = the most important singer
- band = group
- choir = group of singers (in church)
- old / the eldest
- young / the youngest

PREPARE YOUR FINAL TASKS

→ Book p. 105

Speak about the Jackson Five. Talk about their musical style, the way they dressed...

The Jackson Five were 5... They were... Their band was created in... At that time music... Michael Jackson was...

CONSEILS **TICE**

Attention à ne pas parler que de Michael Jackson. Pour t'aider, fais la liste de tous les membres du groupe. Cherche d'autres titres de chanson et écoute-les sur Internet.

5 Nashville: capital of country music

GET READY! → Book p. 106

Read and react.

The Kings of Country: Bob Dylan and Carrie Underwood

Country music combines traditional folk music from the Appalachian Mountains and blues music from the American South. The lyrics are simple, accompanied by the guitar, the banjo, the violin and the harmonica. Nashville, Tennessee is the home of country. Bob Dylan who won the 2016 Nobel Prize for Literature for his lyrics is one famous country singer.

Carrie Underwood is one of the most awarded singers in any genre of music. She has built an international career and won over 100 major awards.

1. Where does country music come from?

a. Country music is...

- [ ] a combination of folk music and rock and roll music.
- [x] a combination of folk music and blues music.
- [ ] a combination of blues music and rock and roll music.

b. It comes from...

- [ ] South America and the Appalachian Mountains.
- [x] the American South and the Appalachian Mountains.

c. What is the home of country music?

Nashville is the home of country music.

2. What instruments can you hear in country music?

I can hear...

- [ ] the guitar, the banjo, the piano and the flute.
- [ ] the banjo, the harmonica, the violin and the cello.
- [x] the guitar, the banjo, the violin and the harmonica.

3. Give the name of two famous country singers.

a. Who are they?

Bob Dylan and Carrie Underwood are two famous singers.

b. What did Bob Dylan receive in 2016?

The Noble Prize for Literature.

c. Why is Carrie Underwood so famous?

- [ ] She is a famous actress too.
- [x] She has won lots of awards.
- [ ] She won British Got Talent.

5 Nashville: capital of country music

GO! VIDEO 19 → Book p. 106

Watch and comment on the video.
Choose between the following exercises (A or B).

AP ACCOMPAGNEMENT PERSONNALISÉ — DIFFÉRENCIATION

CONSEILS
- Regarde la vidéo. Sois attentif
- à ce que dit Carrie Underwood.
- Repère les mots-clefs.

A

First viewing

a. What does she think about the meaning of country music?
She thinks that...
- [ ] writing stories into songs is boring.
- [ ] telling stories on stage is impossible.
- [x] being able to write stories into songs and telling stories is unique to country music.

b. Country music makes it possible...
- [ ] to talk about people's lives.
- [x] to talk about personal things.
- [x] for people to relate to the stories.

c. It explains why...
- [x] people love country music.
- [ ] people hate listening to country music.
- [x] people gravitate towards it.

Second viewing

d. What is a storyteller?
- [x] Someone who tells stories.
- [ ] Someone who reads stories.
- [ ] Someone who copies stories.

e. Complete the sentence.

Country music has ......the best...... ......storytellers...... .

f. What other style of music does she compare country music with?
- [ ] Jazz.
- [x] Gospel.
- [ ] Blues music.

g. Tick the names of two artists she talks about.
- [ ] Bob Dylan.
- [x] Johnny Cash.
- [x] Elvis Presley.
- [ ] Prince.

h. What is country music about?
It is about...
- [ ] peace.
- [x] truth.
- [ ] imaginary things.
- [x] real life.
- [x] singing what you know.

Third viewing

i. What does she want to achieve when she sings?
- [ ] She wants to upset people.
- [x] She doesn't want to shock people.
- [x] She wants her children to listen to her songs.

j. Right or wrong?

	Right	Wrong
– She hopes people will still like her when her children are older.	✔	☐
– She hopes people will say she was a controversial artist.	☐	✔
– She hopes people will say she was cool.	✔	☐

CONSEILS
- Lis les questions avant de regarder la vidéo,
- tu pourras alors te concentrer plus facilement
- sur les points qui te sont demandés. Tu peux
- relire le vocabulaire des leçons précédentes.

Vocabulary
- **upset** = make someone unhappy
- **relate** to = identify with
- **achieve** = accomplish

B

First viewing

What does she think about the meaning of country music?

a. Circle the words you hear.

(able) / (write) / (read) / (stories) / histories / (songs) / sings / (telling) / (unique) / technique / county / (country).

b. Complete the sentence: She thinks that country music is...

being able to write stories. Telling stories is unique to country music.

c. What does it explain?

People love country music

because it tells real stories.

Second viewing

Say what you understand about her opinion on this music.

d. What is a storyteller? A storyteller is someone...

who tells stories.

e. Complete the sentence: Country

music has the best storytellers

f. What other style of music does she compare country music to?

She compares country music to gospel music.

g. Then she mentions two artists: Name them.

Elvis Presley

and Johnny Cash.

h. What is country music about? Circle the words you can hear.

Peace / (truth) / imaginary things / (real life) / fiction / (about singing what you know).

i. Sum up Carrie Underwood's definition of country music using everything she said.

Country music is about truth, real life, about singing what you know, about writing and telling stories, about personal things.

Third viewing

j. What does she want to achieve when she sings her songs?

She doesn't want

to shock people.

She wants her children

to listen to her songs.

k. Sum up two things she says about the future:

– She hopes people will still

like her when her children are older.

– She hopes people will say

she was cool.

6 Queen B. and Houston

GET READY!

→ Book p. 107

Look and react.

1. Who is this woman?

a. This is...

- [ ] Shakira.
- [x] Beyoncé.
- [ ] Rihanna.

b. Her real name is...

- [x] Giselle Knowles.
- [ ] Isabel Mebarak.
- [ ] Robyn Fenti.

2. What do you know about her?

a. She is...

- [ ] an actress and a singer.
- [ ] a singer and a songwriter.
- [x] a singer, a songwriter, a dancer and an actress.

b. What's her nationality?
She is...

- [x] American.
- [ ] Egyptian.

c. What is her music style?
She sings...

- [ ] opera.
- [x] RnB, pop, funk and soul music.
- [ ] Spanish music.

d. She was a member of...

- [ ] the Spice Girls.
- [x] Destiny's Child.
- [ ] TLC.

GO!

→ Book p. 107

Growing up in Houston

Growing up in Houston was fun. We always had a huge backyard to play in. My mom allowed my friends to come over all the time; it was like a continuous slumber party[1] at our house. I spent my summers going to AstroWorld (a theme park), SplashTown (a family water park), Ms. Darlett's dance class & showcases[2]. I had a great childhood in Houston!

When I come home to Houston, I go straight to my mom's house to eat some home cooked food. I love to go to my church St. John's on West Gray and go up to my management company Music World Entertainment. [...]

I would have to say some of my favorite memories of Houston are performing at my mother's hair salon and the music showcases we entered trying to get discovered. I can recall how hard my mother and father worked scheduling[3] rehearsals[4], designing costumes and booking[5] shows. Houston is where my stage presence and confidence[6] was developed. [...]

www.visithoustontexas.com

1. soirée pyjama - 2. présentation / démonstration - 3. prévoir - 4. répétitions - 5. réservant - 6. assurance.

CONSEILS

Avant de lire le texte, fais l'exercice de vocabulaire. Il va te permettre de mieux comprendre ce que tu vas lire. Lis le texte plusieurs fois, souligne les mots que tu ne comprends pas puis réponds aux questions.

1. Match the words from the text to their synonyms.

1. grow up	a. scene
2. huge	b. back garden
3. backyard	c. get older
4. come over	d. execute
5. childhood	e. remember
6. perform	f. youth
7. recall	g. immense
8. stage	h. visit

2. Read and comment on the text. Choose between the following exercises (A or B).

AP ACCOMPAGNEMENT PERSONNALISÉ

DIFFÉRENCIATION

A

First reading

a. Talk about her childhood.
Where did she grow up?
She grew up in...
- ☐ St John.
- ☑ Houston.
- ☐ West Gray.

b. Did she grow up in a house or in an apartment?

She grew up in ..... a house .....

because they always had a

..... huge backyard ..... to play in.

c. Was she a lonely child?
- ☐ Yes, she was, because her friends rarely visited her.
- ☑ No, she wasn't, because her friends visited her all the time.

d. What did she do in the summer?
She went...
- ☐ surfing.
- ☑ to entertainment parks.

e. She took...
- ☑ dance lessons.
- ☐ cooking lessons.

Second reading

f. What about today? Does she still live in Houston today?
- ☐ Yes, she does.
- ☑ No, she doesn't.

g. Where does she go first when she comes back to Houston?
She goes...
- ☐ to her childhood's house.
- ☑ to her mum's house.
- ☐ to her old school.

h. Where else does she go?
She also goes to...
- ☐ her friends'.
- ☑ her church.
- ☐ Ms Darlett's.
- ☑ her management company.

Third reading

i. Talk about her best memories.
Her best memories were...
- ☐ when she went to the entertainment parks.
- ☑ when she made a show at her mother's job.
- ☐ when she had slumber parties with her friends.
- ☑ when she went to music showcases.

j. What did her parents do for her?
They...
- ☑ helped her launch/start her career.
- ☐ bought her a magnificent house.
- ☐ sent her to a very good school.

k. What did she get in Houston?
She got...
- ☑ confidence.
- ☐ fame.
- ☐ power.

l. And she developed her...
- ☑ presence
- ☐ absence

on stage.

Queen B. and Houston

B

First reading

a. Talk about her childhood. Where did she grow up?

She grew up in Houston.

b. Did she grow up in a house or in an apartment?

She grew up in a house because they always had a huge backyard to play in.

c. Was she a lonely child?

No, she wasn't, because her mom allowed her friends to come over all the time. It was like a continuous slumber party at their house.

d. What did she do in the summer?

She went to Astro World and Splash Town and took dance lessons.

CONSEILS

Fais bien attention au découpage du texte, cela t'aidera à répondre aux différentes étapes de la grille.

Second reading

e. What about today? Does she still live in Houston?

No, she doesn't.

f. Where does she go first when she comes back to Houston?

She goes to her mum's house because she loves home cooked food.

g. Where else does she go?

She also goes to her church and her management company Music World Entertainment.

Vocabulary

- church = religious place to pray
- enter**tain**ment park = amusement park

Third reading

h. Talk about her best memories.

Her best memories were when she performed at her mother's hair salon and at the music showcases dance lessons.

i. What did her parents do for her? They...

- [x] helped her launch/start her career.
- [ ] bought her a magnificent house.
- [ ] sent her to a very good school.

j. What did she get in Houston?

She got her stage presence and her confidence.

PREPARE YOUR FINAL TASKS

→ Book p. 107

Talk about Beyoncé's childhood.
Talk about what she did with her friends and with her parents.
Talk about the beginning of her career in Houston.
When she was young, Beyoncé lived in... She had... Every summer she went... She also attended...

CONSEILS

Aide-toi du texte pour préparer ce que tu vas dire, mais attention à ne pas répéter ce que tu as lu !

L'expression de la volonté avec *want* au prétérit → Book p. 109

Want est toujours suivi de l'infinitif complet (*to* + BV).

Ex.: I wanted to be with you.

Lorsqu'il y a un complément, il se place avant *to* + BV.

Ex.: I wanted you to be happy.

1 Forme des phrases avec *want* au prétérit pour parler de Prince.

a. When he was young, Prince (want / be) a singer.

When he was young, Prince wanted to be a singer.

b. His father (want / him / do) all the things he had not been able to do during his youth.

His father wanted him to do all the things he had not been able to do during his youth.

c. As an adult he (want / his fans / call) him Prince, Love Symbol or TAFKAP (for "the artist formerly known as Prince").

As an adult he wanted his fans to call him Prince, Love Symbol or TAFKAP (for "the artist formerly known as Prince").

d. In his songs, he (want / celebrate) his birth town, Minneapolis.

In his songs, he wanted to celebrate his birth town, Minneapolis.

e. Prince (want / be) as famous as Michael Jackson.

Prince wanted to be as famous as Michael Jackson.

2 Remets les mots dans l'ordre.

a. always / Prince / dresses / wear / and / wanted / to / extravagant / make-up.

Prince always wanted to wear extravagant dresses and make-up.

b. to / wanted / recognized / by / other / be / profesionnal / the / he / singers.

He wanted to be recognized by the other profesionnal singers.

c. his / wanted / Tyka / sister / to / too / play / music.

His sister Tyka wanted to play music too.

Le present perfect → Book p. 109

Pour parler d'une action passée qui a une conséquence dans le présent,

pour faire le bilan d'une action passée ou pour parler d'une action passée qui est encore en cours dans le présent, j'utilise le *present perfect*.

Forme affirmative : S + have + BV.

Forme négative : S + have + not + BV.

Pour les verbes réguliers, j'utilise : -ed.

Pour les verbes irréguliers : je les apprends par cœur.

3 Remets les mots dans l'ordre.

a. Carrie Underwood / songs / written / lots of / has.

Carrie Underwood has written lots of songs.

b. has / over / won / awards / she / 100.

She has won over 100 awards.

c. been / she / a / has / very / artist / successful.

She has been a very successful artist.

d. an / career / has / she / built / international / the years / over.

She has built an international career over the years.

e. has / she / in / Nashville / lived.

She has lived in Nasville.

"Is there any Motown song that you don't use in your aerobics class?"

La prononciation de la lettre « o » → Book p. 110

41 CD2 91 MP3

1 Écoute les mots suivants et classe-les dans la bonne colonne.

one / money / two / show / go / don't / shoes / do / to / off / knock / over / honey / on

[ʌ]	[uː]	[ɒ]	[əʊ]
one	shoes	off	over
money	to	knock	show
honey	two	on	go
	do		don't

Les sons [ʊ] et [uː] → Book p. 110

2 Écoute les mots suivants et classe-les dans la bonne colonne. 43 CD2 93 MP3

Houston / music / huge / cooked / food / scheduling / childhood / costume / booking

[ʊ]	[uː]
cooked	Houston
childhood	music
booking	huge
	scheduling
	costume
	food

Auto-évaluation

→ Book p. 114

Connaissances et compétences linguistiques

Vocabulary

- Je connais le vocabulaire de la musique.

Grammar

- Je sais parler de la volonté au prétérit.
- Je sais utiliser le prétérit simple.
- Je sais utiliser le *present perfect*.

Phonology

- Je sais prononcer les différents sons de la lettre « o ».
- Je sais prononcer le [uː] et le [ʊ].

Compétences langagières et domaines du socle commun

Écouter et comprendre
Domaines 1, 2

- Je sais comprendre une vidéo.

Lire et comprendre
Domaines 1, 2

- Je sais lire et comprendre une chanson.
- Je sais repérer les informations essentielles d'un document extrait d'un site Internet.

Parler en continu
Domaines 1, 2, 3

- Je sais donner des informations sur une période musicale et sur des chanteurs précis.

Écrire
Domaines 1,2,5

- Je sais rédiger un texte sur un chanteur, une chanteuse ou un groupe en particulier.

Réagir et dialoguer
Domaines 1,2

- Je sais exprimer mes goûts et sentiments sur une chanson, un chanteur, un style musical...

PEAC

Culture et Parcours
Domaines 1, 2, 3, 5

- Je connais les différents styles de musique qui existent aux États-Unis.
- Je connais les différentes périodes musicales.

8 Growing up in India

1 School on a bus

GET READY! → Book p. 116

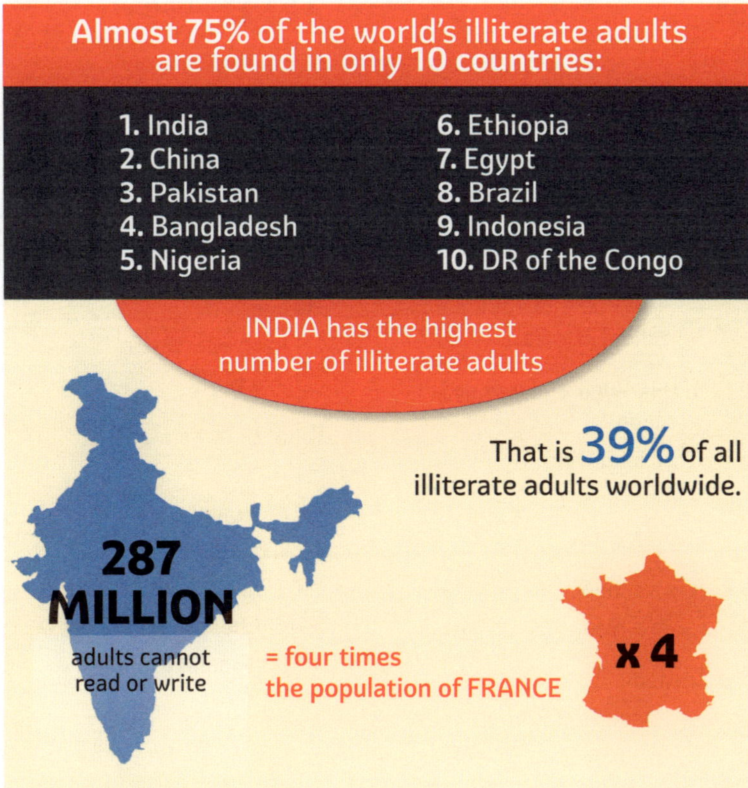

1. Look at the document and react. What it is about?

a. It is about...

- [x] India.
- [ ] China.
- [ ] France.

b. It is also about...

- [ ] adults who can't sing.
- [ ] adults who can't dance.
- [x] adults who can't read or write.

c. How are they called?

They are called ......illiterate...... adults.

2. Give information about India. Tick the correct answers.

- [x] Illiteracy is most frequent in India, China and Pakistan.
- [ ] Illiteracy is most frequent in France, Canada and England.

- [ ] Pakistan has the biggest number of illiterate adults.
- [x] India has the biggest number of illiterate adults.

- [ ] In India, 287 000 people are illiterate.
- [x] In India, 287 000 000 people are illiterate.

- [ ] France's population = 4 x India.
- [x] India's population = 4 x France.

1 School on a bus

GO! VIDEO 20 → Book p. 116

Watch and comment on the video. Choose between the following exercises (A or B).

AP ACCOMPAGNEMENT PERSONNALISÉ — DIFFÉRENCIATION

CONSEILS
Avant de regarder la vidéo, lis plusieurs fois les questions. Repère les mots-clefs et tente de les retrouver lors de tes visionnages.

A

First viewing

a. Say what you can about the video. It is about...

- [ ] a girl.
- [x] a boy.
- [ ] school in England.
- [x] school in India.

b. In this video, children go to school...

- [ ] in a building.
- [x] on a bus.
- [ ] in a park.

c. It is a school...

- [ ] in a river.
- [x] on wheels.

d. Its name is...

- [x] "Door Step School".
- [ ] "Step by Step School".
- [ ] "The School Next Door".

Second viewing

e. Give information about the boy. The boy lives at a street corner.

(Right) / Wrong.

f. He lives...

- [ ] in an apartment.
- [x] in a tent.

g. What does he own?

- [ ] A TV.
- [ ] A computer.
- [x] A game.
- [ ] Video games.
- [x] Clothes.
- [x] A schoolbag.

Third viewing

h. What can you say about the vehicle in the video? This bus is...

- [ ] small.
- [x] big.
- [ ] black.
- [x] white.

i. On the bus, children can...

- [ ] sleep.
- [x] play.
- [x] study.

j. Teachers also go and work on the bus.

(Right) / Wrong

k. This bus...

- [ ] never moves.
- [x] sometimes goes to pick up children.
- [x] sometimes takes children to school.

B

First viewing

Say what you can about the video.

a. This video is about ....a boy........ and ....school in India........ .

b. Where do children go to school in this video?

Children go to school on a bus.

c. It is a school...

- [ ] in a river.
- [x] on wheels.

d. What is the school's name?

The school's name is "Door Step School".

Second viewing

Give information about the boy.

e. Where does the boy live? He lives at a street corner.

f. Does he live in an apartment or in a tent? He lives in a tent.

g. What does he own?

☐ A TV. ☐ A computer. ☑ A game. ☐ Video games. ☑ Clothes. ☑ A schoolbag.

h. Make a sentence.

He owns a game, clothes and a schoolbag.

Third viewing

What can you say about the vehicle in the video?

i. Describe the bus.

It is big and white.

j. What can children do on the bus?

On the bus children can play and study.

k. Who also goes and works on the bus?

Teachers also go and work on the bus.

l. This bus...

☐ never moves. ☑ sometimes goes to pick up children. ☑ sometimes takes children to school.

CONSEILS

Toutes les réponses aux questions sont dans la vidéo. Concentre-toi sur les mots qui te semblent familiers. Relis le vocabulaire du manuel. Sois attentif à l'environnement du garçon. Repère les différences entre ce que tu connais et ce qu'il vit.

Vocabulary

- **illi**teracy = inability to read and write
- wheels: *les roues*
- street **cor**ner: *intersection*
- own: *posséder*

2 BK Birla School

GET READY! VIDEO 21

→ Book p. 117

Watch the video and answer the questions.

1. What is this document about?

- [x] A typical day at the Indian school "BK Birla Centre for Education".
- [ ] A typical day at the American school "BK Birla Centre for Education".
- [ ] A typical day at the English school "BK Birla Centre for Education".

2. Describe a typical day there. Tick the correct sentences.

- [ ] It is a school.
- [x] It is a boarding school.

- [x] Students get up at 5.40 am and practice yoga.
- [ ] Students get up at 6.40 am and practice karate.

- [ ] After breakfast, they go to class.
- [x] After breakfast and Assembly, they go to class.

- [x] They have 8 periods between 8.50 am and 1.55 pm.
- [ ] They have 4 periods between 8.00 am and 11.55 am.

- [x] After lunch, they have prep, they play games and sports and they have a snack.
- [ ] After lunch, they play games and practice sports and have a snack.

- [ ] Before dinner, students relax and play video games.
- [x] Before dinner, students study again (at the library, at the robotics lab, at the study hall...).

- [ ] Before going to bed, they study again.
- [x] Before going to bed, they have free time.

GO! → Book p. 117

Read and write.

CONSEILS

- Concentre-toi sur les mots que tu connais déjà et aide-toi des mots transparents. Relève les mots qui reviennent souvent et note ceux que tu ne comprends pas.

www.bkbirlacentre.com

BK Birla Centre for Education is considered among the best boarding schools in India. To ensure[1] this, the school adopts the following code, which every student has to follow strictly.
The school uniform must be worn[2] on all working days.
Each student must be punctual and regular in attendance.
Changing of classrooms between periods should be done in silence and in an orderly manner.
Care should be taken of class furniture namely[3] computers, cupboards, desks and chairs.
Valuable articles should not be brought to school.
Students must converse in English at all times.
Student must not be rude/disobedient to teachers.
Students should not miss any teaching/games/activity period.
Students should keep their bed tidy[4].
Students should not play with ball/racquet/bat/hockey stick in the dormitories and corridors.

1. garantir, assurer – 2. porté – 3. à savoir – 4. rangé, ordonné

Read and comment on the text. Choose between the following exercises (A or B).

AP ACCOMPAGNEMENT PERSONNALISÉ

DIFFÉRENCIATION

A

First reading

a. Read the text and react. What is this document?

- [ ] It is BK Birla Centre for Education's timetable.
- [x] It is BK Birla Centre for Education's code of conduct.

b. It is a list of...

- [ ] students.
- [x] rules.
- [ ] school subjects.

c. All the students must respect the school's code of conduct.

(Right) / Wrong

Second reading

Give information about the rules at BK Birla School.

d. The students should always respect the rules...

- [x] in the classrooms.
- [x] in the corridors.
- [x] in the dormitories.

e. They should wear a uniform on all working days.

(Right) / Wrong

f. They should always...

- [x] be polite and respectful.
- [ ] be late.
- [ ] be impolite/rude.
- [x] be quiet and punctual.
- [ ] be disobedient.
- [x] be obedient.

Third reading

g. Say what the students should not do. Tick the correct answers.

- [x] They shouldn't destroy school furniture.
- [ ] They shouldn't respect school furniture.
- [x] They shouldn't speak any languages except English.
- [ ] They shouldn't bring books to school.
- [x] They shouldn't bring objects of value to school.
- [x] They shouldn't disobey the teachers.
- [x] They shouldn't miss a class.
- [ ] They shouldn't go to all the classes.
- [ ] They shouldn't make their beds.
- [x] They shouldn't forget to make their beds.

B

First reading

a. Read the text and react. What is this document?

It is BK Birla Centre for Education's code of conduct.

b. Is it a list of students, rules or school subjects? It is a list of rules.

c. Who must respect the school's code of conduct?

Every student must respect the school's code of conduct.

Second reading

Give information about the rules at BK Birla School.

d. Where should the students always respect the rules?

They should respect the rules in the classrooms, in the corridors and in the dormitories.

e. What should the students wear on all working days?

They should always wear a uniform.

f. They should always...

- [x] be polite.
- [x] be respectful.
- [ ] be late.
- [ ] be impolite / rude.
- [ ] be disagreeable.
- [x] be quiet.
- [x] be punctual.
- [ ] be agitated.
- [ ] be disobedient.
- [x] be obedient.

Third reading

g. Say what the students should not do. Choose from the list below and make sentences.

destroy school furniture / respect school furniture / speak English only / speak any languages except English / bring books to school / bring objects of value to school / obey the teachers / disobey the teachers / miss a class / go to all the classes / make their beds / forget to make their beds / play sports inside the dormitories and corridors / play sports on the games field.

CONSEILS

Lis très attentivement les questions et souligne les mots que tu ne connais pas. Souviens-toi de ce que tu as vu dans la première séquence, sur l'école.

Vocabulary

- **boa**rding school = school where you study, sleep and stay the week
- prep = homework
- school **fur**niture = objects for school like tables, desks...
- **ru**les = code of conduct
- be diso**be**dient = not obey
- **obey** = follow orders

PREPARE YOUR FINAL TASKS

→ Book p. 117

Talk about the rules at BK Birla Centre and say what pupils should do or shouldn't do.

They shouldn't be late and they should go to all classes. / They shouldn't destroy school furniture...

CONSEILS

Souviens-toi des codes de conduite vus lors de la première séquence sur l'école. Essaie de noter les différences et les similitudes.

3 Girls at school

GET READY!

→ Book p. 118

Look and react.

1. Describe the picture.

a. What can you see?

- [ ] Girls in a park.
- [x] Girls at school.
- [ ] Boys and girls at work.

b. What are they wearing?

- [x] A uniform. - [ ] A costume. - [ ] Casual clothes.

c. How do they look?

- [ ] Sad and disappointed.
- [x] Happy and excited.
- [ ] Serious and strict.

2. Read the text below and explain the differences between a boy's education and a girl's education in India.

In India, girls are expected to become wives, daughters-in-law and mothers. They get married at a young age and it is hard for them to get an education. For boys, it is different, they can get married later and are trained to get a job.

a. Say what girls are expected to do in India.

They are expected to...
- [ ] get a good school education.
- [x] become a good wife, mother and daughter-in law.
- [ ] get a well-paid job.

b. What about boys in India?

They are trained to...
- [ ] become good husbands, fathers and sons-in-law.
- [x] get a job.
- [ ] go to university.

c. Right or wrong?

– Girls in India have the same chances as boys in their education. Wrong

– Girls marry at a young age in India. Right

– Girls can go to school easily. Wrong

GO!

→ Book p. 118

Read and understand.

CONSEILS

- Lis le texte attentivement. Relève les mots-clefs
- qui sont porteurs de sens comme *want, will*…
- Note tous les mots que tu ne comprends pas.

Adapted from: www.goingtoschool.com

Baby Kumari, Age 15
Maharani Janaki Kuwar High School

Baby Kumari has two more names. Her real name is Bharti and her family and friends call her Raunak (joy or light). [...] Baby's mother wants her to live a different life from [...] other girls in the village, [...] not to stop her studies, not to get married, not to make the same mistake as she did, of not studying further. [...] Baby wants to become a police officer because she wants to do something for India. [...] "In order to become a police officer [...] I have to study hard, I should be able to think differently; [...] I may not get support from my family, but I will not stop trying".

She doesn't understand why in her village, girls' parents do not want them to study after Grade 10 or why they get married after that. [...] "My mother encourages me but not my father. My brothers get to study, I wish our guardians supported us".

Read and comment on the text. Choose between the following exercises (A or B).

ACCOMPAGNEMENT PERSONNALISÉ AP

DIFFÉRENCIATION

A

First reading

a. Who is the text about? What is the girl's complete name?

[ ] Baby Kumari. [ ] Bharti Raunak Kumari. [x] Baby Barty Raunak Kumari.

b. How old is she? She is 15 years old.

c. Give the name of her school. Maharani Janaki Kuwar High School.

d. What does her mother want her to do?

She wants her to...

- [x] live a different life from hers.
- [ ] have the same life as the other girls in the village.
- [ ] stop her studies.
- [x] carry on with her studies.
- [ ] get married after finishing her studies.

e. What does she tell her not to do?

She tells her not to...

- [x] get married at a young age.
- [x] make the same mistakes as she did.
- [ ] continue her studies.
- [ ] study further.

Second reading

f. What does she want to become when she is older? Right or Wrong.
- She wants to get married after Grade 10. Wrong
- She wants to become a police officer. Right
- She wants to stop studying. Wrong

g. Say why she wants to become a police officer.
- [ ] She wants to fight crime.
- [x] She wants to do something for India.

h. Say what she has to do.
- [x] Work very hard.
- [ ] Get her mother's support.
- [ ] Get married.

Vocabulary
- light = luminosity
- mis**ta**ke = error
- in **or**der to become a police **o**fficer
- study **fur**ther = study more
- sup**port** = help
- try = attempt

Third reading

i. What difficulties does she encounter? Right or Wrong.
- Her mother supports her. Right
- Her father encourages her. Wrong
- In India, girls' parents want their daughters to get married early. Right
- They think girls don't need an education. Right

j. Read the whole text again and circle the words describing Baby's personality.

(optimistic) – (determined) – sad – (courageous) – (intelligent) – pessimistic – lazy – (hopeful).

CONSEILS
Relis le texte plusieurs fois pour t'aider à répondre aux questions. Concentre-toi sur ce que raconte Baby à propos de l'école. Reprends le vocabulaire déjà vu et les mots que tu as notés. Cherche leur définition pour t'aider.

B

First reading

a. Who is the text about? What is the girl's complete name?

Her complete name is Baby Barty Raunak Kumari

b. How old is she? She is 15 years old.

c. What school does she go to?

She goes to Maharani Janaki Kuwar High School.

d. What does her mother want her to do?

Her mother wants her to live a different life and to carry on with her studies.

e. What does she tell her not to do?

She tells her not to get married at a young age and not to make the same mistakes as she did.

Second reading

f. What does she want to become when she is older? Right or Wrong.

– She wants to get married after Grade 10. Wrong

– She wants to become a police officer. Right

– She wants to stop studying. Wrong

g. Say why she wants to become a police officer.

She wants to do something for her country.

h. Say what she has to do.

– She has to work very hard and get her father's support.

Third reading

i. What difficulties does she encounter? Right or Wrong. Justify your answers.

– Her mother supports her. Right / line 2 and line 8.

– Her father encourages her. Wrong / line 8

– In India, girls' parents want their daughters to get married early. Right / line 8

j. Read the whole text again and circle the words describing Baby's personality.

optimistic – determined – sad – courageous – intelligent – pessimistic – strong – lazy – hard-working

k. Write a sentence using these words to describe Baby's personality. Justify your answer.

Baby has a strong personality, she is hard-working and determined. She is also very courageous and optimistic. She wants to achieve her dreams.

4 Hobbies in India

GET READY!

→ Book p. 119

Read and react.

www.mumbaitheatreguide.com

Growing Up[1] is a story about a group of children - Sonia, Isha, Vivi and Nikhil on their exciting journey[2] through Puberty. They are all going through various physical and emotional changes and are confused.

1. grandir - 2. voyage

1. Say what you can about the document.

a. It is...
☐ a leaflet for a show. ☑ a website page. ☐ the cover of a magazine.

b. What is the name of the website? It is ....Mumbai Theatre guide........ .com

c. What is the page about?
It is about... ☑ a play. ☐ a movie. ☐ a novel.

d. What is the title of the play? The title is ....Growing Up........

2. Who and what can you see?

a. I can see... ☐ boys and girls. ☐ adults and children. ☑ a man and teenagers.

b. Who are they?
They are... ☑ actors and actresses. ☑ characters of the play. ☐ spectators.

c. I can also read... ☑ a synopsis of the play. ☐ a scene from the play. ☐ an act from the play.

d. What is the play about?
The play is about... ☐ a group of teenagers at school.
☑ a group of teenagers experiencing puberty.
☐ a group of teenagers as they enter middle school.

4 Hobbies in India

GO! → Book p. 119

Read the text and do the exercices.

CONSEILS

Concentre-toi sur le vocabulaire que tu connais déjà. Lis attentivement le texte. Prends des notes et souligne les mots que tu ne comprends pas.

www.timesofindia.indiatimes.com

Learning hobbies the fun way

BANGALORE: A group of students learning dance in a room, another bunch[1] focusing on their karate kicks. Some design paper lamps even as others practise their notes on various instruments. It's no hobby centre but the scene at Podar International School twice a week.

Wednesdays and Fridays are special for students. For an hour and 40 minutes, all the students are engrossed[2] in fun activities of their choice. The school has made it mandatory[3] for every child to learn two hobbies and they have a wide range[4] to choose from.

Principal Narayana Joisa believes helping children acquire life skills[5] is important. "While everybody is busy producing rank holders, we prepare students to be smart so they can take on the world", she says.

Santrupti Rajankar, October 28th 2013

1. groupe - 2. absorbés - 3. obligatoire - 4. large éventail - 5. compétences

1. Match the words to their synonyms.

1. bunch	a. conquer the world
2. focus	b. obligatory
3. twice	c. intelligent
4. engrossed in	d. group
5. mandatory	e. competence
6. wide	f. concentrate
7. range	g. captivated by
8. skill	h. large
9. smart	i. domain
10. take on the world	j. on two occasions

2. Now read and comment on the text. Choose between the following exercises (A or B).

AP ACCOMPAGNEMENT PERSONNALISÉ — DIFFÉRENCIATION

A

First reading

a. What sort of document is it? Its is...

☐ a newspaper article. ☐ a synopsis for a new novel. ☑ an article from a website.

b. Who wrote it?

☑ Santrupti Rajankar. ☐ Narayana Joisa. ☐ Chandra Bhattacharjee.

c. When was it published?

It was published on... ☐ November 13th 2008. ☑ October 28th 2013. ☐ December 28th 2016.

Second reading

d. What it is about? It is about...

☐ students learning new sports.
☑ students learning hobbies at school.
☐ students learning new subjects at school.

e. Where does it take place?

In... ☐ Mumbai. ☐ New Delhi. ☑ Bangalore.

f. What is the name of the school?

☐ Poudlard International School. ☐ Pool International School.
☑ Podar International School.

Third reading

What hobbies can the students practice?

g. How many hobbies do they have to choose? ☐ 3. ☐ 4. ☑ 2.

h. It is... ☑ mandatory. ☐ unnecessary.

i. About the hobbies they can choose...

☑ they have a wide selection of hobbies. ☐ their choice is restricted.

j. Give examples of the hobbies they can practice.

They ......can practice dance, karate, music...... .

k. When do the students learn these new hobbies?

☐ Once a week, on Wednesday. ☑ Twice a week, on Wednesday and Friday.

l. How long does each lesson last?

☑ An hour and forty minutes. ☐ An hour and a half. ☐ An hour and fourteen minutes.

m. Do the students like learning these new activities?

Yes, they do. ....

n. Why do they like doing these hobbies?

☑ Because they are fun activities. ☐ Because they are boring activities.

4 Hobbies in India

CONSEILS

Il y a beaucoup d'informations dans le texte. Classe ces informations en différentes catégories (loisirs, horaires, etc.) pour t'aider à mieux comprendre.

B

First reading

a. What sort of document is it? It is an article from a website.

b. Who wrote it? Santrupti Rajankar wrote it.

c. When was it published? It was published on October 28th 2013.

Second reading

d. What is it about? It is about students learning hobbies at school.

e. Where does it take place? It takes place in Bangalore.

f. What is the name of the school? The school is named Podar International School.

Third reading

g. How many hobbies do they have to choose?

They have to choose 2 hobbies, because it is mandatory.

h. Are there many hobbies to choose? They have a wide range to choose from.

i. Give examples of the hobbies they can practice.

They can practice dance, karate, music...

j. When do the students learn these new hobbies?

They learn these hobbies twice a week, on Wednesday and Friday.

k. How long does each activity last?

Each activity lasts an hour and forty minutes.

l. Do the students like learning these new activities? Yes, they do.

m. Why do they like doing these hobbies?

They like doing these hobbies because these activities are fun.

Vocabulary

- **jour**ney = trip
- **bu**sy = occupied
- grow **up** = become an adult, develop into

PREPARE YOUR FINAL TASKS

→ Book p. 119

Explain why the students at Podar International School are lucky.

The students are lucky because... They like doing...

CONSEILS

Pour préparer ton explication, utilise : *like ; enjoy* + BV-*ing*.

5 Indian B-Boys

GET READY!

→ Book p. 120

1. Who can you see?

I can see...

[x] a boy. [ ] a girl. [x] a teenager. [ ] an adult.

2. What is he doing?

a. He is...

[ ] running. [ ] dancing. [x] breakdancing.

b. Where do you think he is?

In the picture, he is...

[x] in the street.
[ ] in a room.
[ ] in a cinema.

c. In the background, we can see...

[x] a wall, outside. [ ] the sea.
[ ] the mountains. [ ] a house.

GO! VIDEO 22

→ Book p. 120

Before watching the video do the following exercise.

1. Match the following words to their synonyms.

1. cramped	a. slum
2. crowded	b. full of people
3. poverty	c. rob/hold up
4. escape	d. run away
5. be committed to	e. original
6. steal	f. equal
7. compete	g. very small
8. ghetto	h. be engaged in/on
9. counterpart	i. take part in
10. funky	j. indigence

ACCOMPAGNEMENT PERSONNALISÉ AP
DIFFÉRENCIATION

2. Now watch and comment on the video.
Choose between the following exercises (A or B).

A

First viewing

a. Who is the video about? It is about...
- ☐ an American boy.
- ☐ an English boy.
- ☑ an Indian boy.

b. His name is...
- ☑ Pankaj.
- ☐ Patrick.
- ☐ Paddington.

c. He is...
- ☐ eight years old.
- ☐ eighty years old.
- ☑ eighteen years old.

d. He is...
- ☐ a schoolboy.
- ☑ a student.
- ☐ a teacher.

e. He lives in...
- ☑ a Mumbai crowded slum.
- ☐ in Mumbai.
- ☐ in New Dehli.

f. He is passionate about...
- ☑ American Hip Hop and breakdance.
- ☐ classical dance.
- ☐ movies.

g. He...
- ☐ sings all the time.
- ☑ dances all the time.
- ☐ runs all the time.

Second viewing

What does he do with his friends?

h. To practice breakdancing, he goes with his friends...
- ☑ in an old fort.
- ☐ in a park.
- ☐ in a dance room.

i. With his friends they call themselves...
- ☐ the Slumdogs.
- ☑ the Slumgods.
- ☐ the Slumboys.

j. They are also called the...
- ☐ D-boys.
- ☑ B-boys.
- ☐ C-boys.

k. It means the...
- ☐ dancing boys.
- ☑ breakdancing boys.
- ☐ charming boys.

Third viewing

l. Why do they do that? They want to prove that the slums are not synonymous with...
- ☑ poverty and a desire to escape.
- ☐ liberty and a desire to move away.
- ☐ fantasy and a desire to leave.

m. For them, breakdancing is a chance to compete for...
- ☐ medals.
- ☑ cash and glory.
- ☐ honors.
- ☑ competitions and playing in Bollywood films.
- ☐ their country.

CONSEILS

Lis les questions plusieurs fois avant de regarder la vidéo. Concentre-toi sur les personnes et les lieux. Tu peux relire l'exercice de vocabulaire, il t'aidera à mieux comprendre la vidéo. Souviens-toi du vocabulaire vu dans les leçons précédentes.

Vocabulary

- in the **back**ground = things at the back
- **us**ed to = accustomed to

B

CONSEILS

Lorsque tu regardes la vidéo, n'hésite pas à noter les termes que tu ne comprends pas. Lors de la correction des exercices, écoute bien les réponses et n'hésite pas à participer.

First viewing

Who is the video about?

a. Who is the young boy? He is an Indian boy.

b. What is his name? His name is Pankaj.

c. How old is he? He is 18 years old.

d. What does he do? He is a student.

e. Where does he live? He lives in a Mumbai crowded slum.

f. What is he passionate about? He is passionate about American Hip Hop and breakdance but he can't dance at home because it is cramped/too small.

Second viewing

What does he do with his friends?

g. Where does he go with his friends to practice breakdancing?

He goes in an old fort with his friends.

h. How do they call themselves?

They call themselves the Slumgods.

i. What is their other name?

They are also called the B-boys as the breakdancing boys.

Third viewing

j. Why do they do that? They want to prove that the slums are not synonymous with...

- [x] poverty and a desire to escape.
- [ ] liberty and a desire to move away.
- [ ] fantasy and a desire to leave.

k. Before practicing breakdance, they used to...

- [x] drink, get into fights and steal.
- [ ] play football every day.
- [ ] stay at home and watch TV.

l. For them breakdancing is a chance to compete for...

- [x] cash and glory.
- [ ] honors.
- [x] competitions and playing in Bollywood films.
- [ ] their country.

6 Kids for Tigers' Fest

GET READY!

→ Book p. 121

Look at the documents and answer the questions.

1. Look at the children.

a. What do they have on their faces?

- [ ] Masks.
- [ ] Glasses.
- [x] Face paint.

b. What documents are these?

- [ ] Pictures in a magazine.
- [x] Screenshots from a video.
- [ ] Extracts from a movie.

2. Which animal do you recognize?

a. It is...

- [ ] A lion.
- [x] A tiger.
- [ ] An eagle.
- [x] A leopard.

b. What is the occasion?

- [x] A festival.
- [ ] A carnival.
- [ ] New Year celebrations.

GO! VIDEO 23

→ Book p. 121

Watch and comment on the video. Choose between the following exercises (A or B).

ACCOMPAGNEMENT PERSONNALISÉ AP

DIFFÉRENCIATION

A

First viewing

a. Say what this document is about.

It is...

- [x] A news report on an event in Mumbai.
- [ ] A documentary on tigers in India.
- [ ] A documentary on a school in India.

b. What is the event about? Circle the words you can hear.

campaign – lions – fest – tigers – awareness – increase – garner – gain – raise – report – rise – organized – association – support – festival – conservation.

CONSEILS

Regarde la vidéo trois fois. Sois attentif aux images pour repérer les lieux et ce qui se passe. Note les mots-clefs.

c. Finish the sentence using the words you circled above.

The video talks about a campaign to increase awareness for tigers' preservation.

d. What is the the name of the fest. It is: the Kids for tigers' fest in Mumbai.

e. What is the name of the campaign? It is: Save our tigers campaign.

Second viewing

f. Write about the organization's objective. What do they want young people to understand?

- [ ] It is not important to protect the tigers.
- [x] Protecting the tigers is protecting their country.
- [x] They have to protect this world.
- [ ] Tigers are dangerous animals.

g. Say how many students attended the event.

- [ ] 12 000.
- [x] 1 200.
- [ ] 120.

Vocabulary

- the aim = the goal

h. Where did they come from?

- [ ] Various schools from India.
- [x] Various schools from Mumbai.
- [ ] Various schools from around the world.

Third viewing

Talk about the activities at the event.

i. Circle the words you hear.

taking pictures – poster making – wearing make-up – fancy dress competition – going to a zoo – going on nature trails – watching cartoons – watching wildlife movies.

j. Complete the sentence with the words you circled above.

The students were involved in poster making, fancy dress competitions, going on nature trails, watching wildlife movies.

k. What is the aim of the fest?

- [ ] To make students understand that tigers must not be protected.
- [x] To make students become ambassadors of the environment's protection.
- [x] To make students raise their voices for the tigers at a young age.
- [ ] To make the elders understand that the tigers don't need protection.

B

First viewing

a. Say what this document is about? It is a news report on an event in Mumbai.

b. What is the event about? Circle the words you can hear.

campaign – lions – fest – tigers – awareness – increase – gain – raise – organized – support – festival – conservation

c. Now explain what the event consists in.

This event is a campaign to increase awareness and raise support for tiger's conservation in India.

d. What is the name of the fest?

The name of the fest is "Kids for tigers' fest in Mumbai".

e. What is the name of the campaign?

The name of the campaign is "Save our tigers' campaign".

Second viewing

f. Write about the organization's objective. What do they want young people to understand?

They want young people to understand that protecting the tigers is protecting their world.

They must make the elders understand that it is very important.

g. Say how many students attended the event. 1 200 students attended the event.

Third viewing

h. Talk about the activities at the event. Circle the words you hear.

poster making – fancy dress competition – going to a zoo – going on nature trails – watching wildlife movies

i. What is the aim of the fest?

The students become ambassadors of the tigers' protection.

PREPARE YOUR FINAL TASKS

→ Book p. 121

Write a short text to present the students' action to protect the tigers in India and explain why it is so important for the environment.

The Tigers' Fest took place at... / Students made posters... / They understood...

CONSEILS

Regarde la vidéo encore une fois. Relis ta leçon et reprends les activités du cahier.
Fais une liste des actions menées par les élèves et rédige un texte pour les présenter en utilisant les amorces de phrases.

Les prépositions de lieu → Book p. 123

Pour situer des objets ou des personnes dans l'espace, on utilise les prépositions de lieu suivantes : in / on / at / to / between / from… to… / next to / in front of / behind

1 Choisis la bonne préposition de lieu.

a. (In) / On India, there are lots of illiterate people.

b. The boy in the video goes at / (to) school at / (on) a bus.

c. He doesn't have a television (at) / in home because his family is not rich.

d. Going to / (from) home (to) / from school is sometimes very difficult for Indian children.

2 Complète les phrases avec la bonne préposition de lieu.

a. Indian children should not go to school on a bus.

b. I don't want this boy to have only one game at home.

c. I want Indian children to go from poverty to wealth.

d. The Indian government should help children on the streets.

Exprimer un conseil ou un reproche → Book p. 123

Pour faire une suggestion ou dire ce qui est quasiment obligatoire, j'utilise should + BV .

Ex.: You should talk to your parents about your problems.

Pour exprimer une quasi-interdiction ou pour faire un reproche, j'utilise shouldn't + BV .

Ex.: You shouldn't sleep in class!

3 Complète les phrases avec *should* ou *shouldn't*.

a. At BK Birla Centre for Education, students shouldn't chat in class.

b. They should listen to their teachers and work hard.

c. They shouldn't be violent and disrespectful so they should always be polite.

d. They should always respect the school's code of conduct.

4 **Fais des phrases avec *should* et *shouldn't* à partir des éléments ci-dessous afin de compléter le code de conduite de l'école.**

a. Students at BK Birla Centre for Education / wear proper sports uniforms on the games field.

Students at BK Birla Centre for Education should wear proper sports uniforms on the games field.

b. They / touch electrical installations.

They shouldn't touch electrical installations.

c. They / be quiet and calm in the school.

They should be quiet and calm in the school.

La proposition infinitive avec *want* et *tell* → Book p. 123

Pour dire ce que je veux faire, j'utilise want + (to) verbe à l'infinitif.

Pour dire que je veux que quelqu'un fasse quelque chose, j'utilise le verbe want + nom ou pronom personnel complément + (to) verbe à l'infinitif.

Pour dire à quelqu'un de faire quelque chose, j'utilise le verbe tell + nom ou pronom personnel complément + (to) verbe à l'infinitif.

5 **Relie les phrases entre elles.**

1. Baby wants to — d. become a police officer when she is older.
2. She tells — a. her friends to study before getting married.
3. Baby's mother wants — b. Baby to study further.
4. She wants — c. her daughter not to make the same mistakes as she did.

Les verbes de goût + V-*ing* → Book p. 124

Pour parler de ce que j'aime ou n'aime pas faire j'utilise un verbe ou expression de goût suivi de V-ing. Les verbes de goût sont, par exemple : like / enjoy / appreciate / be fond of / love / dislike / hate.

6 **Remets les mots dans l'ordre.**

a. boys / love / Indian / cricket / playing.

Indian boys love playing cricket.

b. many / hate / wearing / at / students / school / uniform / a / India / in.

Many students hate wearing a uniform at school in India.

c. enjoy / parents / watching / the / "Growing up" / play / many.

Many parents enjoy watching the play "Growing up".

Language practice PHONOLOGY

L'intonation des propositions avec *must* et *should* → Book p. 124

Dans les phrases avec ....must.... et ....should...., l'intonation est ....descendante.....

1 **Entraîne-toi à prononcer les phrases suivantes en faisant attention à l'intonation.**

a. Pupils shouldn't be late for school.
b. They must not drink during the class.
c. They shouldn't talk in class but listen to the teacher.
d. They should be polite.

Les sons [ɑɪ] et [ɪ] → Book p. 124

En anglais, la lettre « i » se prononce soit [ɪ] qui est un son ....court...., soit [ɑɪ] qui est un son ....long.... (diphtongue).

2 **Lis les mots suivants. Souligne en vert quand tu entends le son [ɑɪ], en rouge le son [ɪ].**

drink / listen / fight / polite / during / abusive / violent / desire / illiterate / wildlife / tigers / lions / original.

Auto-évaluation → Book p. 128

Connaissances et compétences linguistiques

Vocabulary

- Je connais le vocabulaire se rapportant à l'école.
- Je connais le vocabulaire se rapportant à l'adolescence.
- Je connais le vocabulaire se rapportant aux passe-temps.
- Je connais le vocabulaire se rapportant à une fête.

Grammar

- Je sais utiliser les prépositions de lieu.
- Je sais utiliser le modal *should* à la forme affirmative et à la forme négative.
- Je sais utiliser *want* et *tell to*.
- Je sais utiliser les verbes et expressions de goût suivis de V-*ing*.

Phonology

- Je sais prononcer l'intonation descendante des phrases avec *must* et *should*.
- Je sais distinguer les sons [ɑɪ] et [ɪ].

Compétences langagières et domaines du socle commun

Écouter et comprendre
Domaines 1, 2
- Je sais comprendre une vidéo.

Lire et comprendre
Domaines 1, 2
- Je sais lire et comprendre les points essentiels d'un texte ou article.
- Je sais repérer les informations essentielles d'un document extrait d'un site Internet.

Parler en continu
Domaines 1, 2, 3
- Je sais raconter ce qui se passe dans une vidéo.

Écrire
Domaines 1, 2
- Je sais écrire un texte court.

Réagir et dialoguer
Domaines 1, 2, 3
- Je sais faire des commentaires sur les différents aspects de la vie des enfants en Inde.

PEAC

Culture et Parcours
Domaines 1, 2, 3, 5
- Je connais différents aspects de la vie des enfants en Inde.
- Je connais le problème des bidonvilles ainsi que les problèmes de scolarisation des filles en Inde.

Vocabulary

Utilise à nouveau le vocabulaire vu au cours de l'année !

1 Let's talk about school

1 **Donne deux éléments d'un uniforme commençant par... :**

a. « T » : tie , trousers

b. « S » : shirt, skirt, shoes

c. « J » : jacket , jumper

2 **Donne le nom de vêtements ou d'accessoires interdits à l'école, commençant par :**

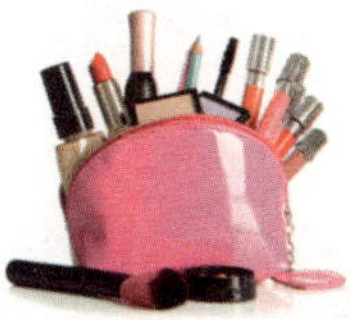

a. « B » : boots

b. « J » : jewellery, jogging

c. « M » : make-up

2 Let's get cooking!

1 **Associe les mots aux images correspondantes.**

chicken breast

cucumber

sweetcorn

lettuce leaves

black pepper

2 **Relie les synonymes entre eux.**

1. cool
2. smooth
3. low-fat
4. skinless
5. chopped
6. soft

a. unctuous
b. reduced-calorie
c. cut into small cubes
d. creamy
e. fresh
f. without the skin

3 New York, New York

1 **Relie les mots aux images correspondantes.**

billboard

bridge

skyscraper

store

harbour

avenue

2 **Trouve les mots correspondants aux définitions suivantes.**

a. You walk on it to cross a river. .... a bridge

b. A place where you can walk and relax in the sun. .... a park

c. A person who walks in the street. .... a pedestrian

d. A very tall building in New York. .... a skyscraper

e. Something you have in your garden. .... plants

4 Once upon a time...

1 **Indique le nom des personnages de contes de fée que tu reconnais.**

an ogre ...... a fairy ...... a king ...... a dwarf

a queen ...... a magician ...... a princess

2 **Trouve le mot qui correspond à chaque définition.**

a. It is a very big imaginary animal that spits fire. .... A dragon

b. This is a man who eats little children. .... An ogre

c. This woman is very nice, she has magic powers. .... A fairy

d. This is a story that ends well, written for children. .... A fairy tale

e. She is the daughter of a king and a queen. .... A princess

Vocabulary

5 Crazy about fashion

1 Fais des phrases à partir des éléments proposés.

Ex.: These women are the most courageous women I know.

Chantelle		the most incredible		
Madeline		the best	woman	in Australia.
Chantelle and Madeline	is	the friendliest	women	in the world.
They	are	the most courageous	model	in Canada.
These top models		the nicest	models	I know.
These women		the most unique		

Chantelle is the nicest model in Canada.

They are the most unique women in the world.

Madeline is the most courageous woman in Australia.

2 Choisis deux images et décris-les. Dis ce que chaque personne porte. Utilise les mots proposés et n'oublie pas les couleurs !

skirt • jeans • a tee shirt • a bag • a blazer • a vest • a scarf • glasses • trousers • a hat • a jacket • socks • high heels • a handbag • a suit • a cardigan • a striped tee shirt • a necklace • flared jeans • a dress • trainers • shoes • high heels • a short • unglasses • a colourful top

6 Long to reign over us

1 **Trouve le mot qui correspond à chaque définition.**

a. This is a feast you celebrate in the street. A street party
b. You use it to pay. A coin
c. He is the son of a king and a queen. A prince
d. This is a special anniversary. A jubilee
e. This person is a queen or a king. A monarch

7 American music

1 **Trouve l'intrus.**

a. a piano – a guitar – a bass – ~~drums~~ – a banjo.
b. a songwriter – a singer – ~~a chef~~ – a musician.
c. ~~an anthem~~ – rock'n roll – soul – jazz – RnB.
d. lyrics – ~~a novel~~ – a verse – a chorus.
e. rhythm – beat – tempo – ~~salsa~~.

8 Growing up in India

1 **Utilise les mots suivants pour résumer l'histoire de Baby.**

Baby • live • India • special • want • study • not get married • young age • hard-working • become • a police officer • older • her mother • support • but • her father • not encourage • in India • girls • not get • education • boys • determined • make • dreams • come true.

Baby lives in India. She is a special girl. She wants to study; she does not want to get married at a young age. She is hard-working; she wants to become a police officer when she is older. Her mother supports her but her father does not encourage her. In India, girls do not get the same education as the boys. But she is determined to make her dreams come true.

Références photos

Couverture *Londres* © Rubén Navarro Pina ; *Shrek* © collection Christophel ; **p. 4** © It's the First Day of School! De Charles M. Schulz/ Happers Collins Publishers ; **p. 7** © Jack Hollingsworth/age footstock ; **p. 11** © Juice Images/Getty Images ; **p. 13** © Cartoon by Nicholson from The Australian www.nicholsoncartoons.com.au ; **p. 16** *haut* © Juice Images/ Getty Images ; *bas 1* © elenovsky/Shutterstock ; *2* © Vector Tradition SM/Shutterstock ; *3* © Africa Studio/Shutterstock ; *4* © elenovsky/Shutterstock ; *5* Mega Pixel/Shutterstock ; *6* Karkas/Shutterstock ; *7* Tarzhanova/Shutterstock ; *8* Tarzhanova/Shutterstock ; **p. 17** © Céline Pesle ; **p. 20** © Jason Sammon/Newspix ; **p. 28** © FOX/Getty Images ; **p. 30** © Andrew John Simpon ; **p. 33** © Penguin Random House ; **p. 34** © Jason Batterham/Shutterstock ; **p. 36** *gauche* Sweetgreen.com/DR ; *droite* © Jeff Morgan 08/Alamy Stock Photo/Photo12 ; **p. 39** © allesalltag/Alamy Stock Photo/Photo12 ; **p. 41** © John Stillwell-WPA Pool/Getty Images ; **p. 46** © Céline Pesle ; **p. 48** © Debbie Egan-Chin/NY Daily News Archive/Getty Images ; **p. 50** © Spencer Grant/Getty Image ; **p. 53** © Céline Pesle ; **p. 56** © Randy Duchaine/Alamy Stock Photo/Photo12 ; **p. 57** © Mike Dotta/Shutterstock ; **p. 58** *haut* © Beth Dixson / Alamy Stock Photo/Photo12 ; *bas* © Philippe Debled/Getty Images ; **p. 59** © Alex Millaueur/Shutterstock ; **p. 66** © Collection Christophel © Relativity Media / Metropolitan Filmexport ; **p. 67** © Collection Christophel © Walt Disney ; **p. 68** © Collection Christophel © Walt Disney; **p. 69** *haut* © Erik Dreyer/Getty Images ; *bas* © Nicescene/Shutterstock ; **p. 72** © Look and Learn / Bridgeman Images ; **p. 76** © Quentin Blake/United Agents ; **p. 80** © Quentin Blake/ United Agents ; **p. 88** *1* © Oxfam/REX/Shutterstock/Sipa ; *2* © Hero Images/Getty Images ; *3* © Stephanie Rausser/Getty Images ; *4* © Robert Daly/Getty Images ; **p. 90** © Anton Oparin / Alamy Stock Photo/Photo12 ; **p. 93** *1* © Gregory Wrona / Alamy Stock Photo/Photo12 ; *2* © Margarethe Wichert/ Getty Images ; *3* © dov makabaw / Alamy Stock Photo/ Photo12 ; *4* © Keith Erskine / Alamy Stock Photo/Photo12 ; **p. 96** *haut* © Pete Souza/Official White House ; *bas 1* © Nisakorn Neera/Shutterstock ; *2* © nikitaglazik/Shutterstock ; *3* © mimo/Shutterstock ; **p. 99** *gauche* © Carlos Alvarez/Getty Images/Afp ; *droite* © Anton Oparin/Alamy Stock Photo/ Photo12 **; p. 101** © DR ; **p. 103** © Everett Collection/Shutterstock ; **p. 108** © Copyright 2015 Graphic News. Reprint by permission only. All rights reserved. ; **p. 110** *1* © Speaight/ Mansell/The LIFE Images Collection/Getty Images ; *2* © Keystone-France/Gamma-Rapho / Getty Images ; *3* © Hulton Archive/Getty Images ; *4* © Getty images 613465294 ; *5* © Tim Graham/Getty Images ; *6* © Danny Martindale/ WireImage/ Getty Images ; *7* © Ute Grabowsky/Photothek/Getty Images ; *8* © Danny Martindale/WireImage/Getty Images ; **p. 113** © The Westminster Collection ; **p. 114** © The Westminster Collection ; **p. 116** *gauche* © Sean Kilpatrick - WPA Pool / Getty Images ; *droite* © Anwar Hussein Collection/ROTA/ WireImage/Getty Images ; **p. 120** *1* © Chris Jackson/Getty Images ; *2* © Featureflash Photo Agency/Shutterstock ; *3* © Featureflash Photo Agency/Shutterstock ; *4* © Anwar Hussein/Getty Images ; *5* © Frederic Legrand/COMEO/Shutterstock ; *6* © Featureflash Photo Agency/Shutterstock ; *7* © Helga Esteb/Shutterstock ; *8* © Helga Esteb/Shutterstock ; *9* © Max Mumby/Indigo/Getty Images ; *10* © Mark Cuthbert/UK Press/Getty Images ; **p. 123** © London News Pictures/REX/Shutterstock/Sipa ; **p. 127** © bibiphoto/Shutterstock ; **p. 130** © Bettmann/Getty Images ; **p. 133** © Ian Dickson/REX/Shutterstock/Sipa ; **p. 135** *1* © Janette Beckman/Getty Images ; *2* © Bob Berg/Getty Images ; *3* © Keith Major/Contour by Getty Images ; *4* © Michael O'Neill/Corbis via Getty Images ; *5* © Aaron Rapoport/Corbis via Getty Images ; **p. 138** *haut* © David Redfern/Redferns/Getty Images ; *bas* © alisafarov/Shutterstock ; **p. 139** © Thinglass/Shutterstock ; **p. 141** *haut gauche* © Elliott Landy/Redferns/Getty Images ; *droite* © Mike Windle/ Getty Images/Afp ; **p. 144** © Larry Busacca/PW/WireImage/Getty Images ; **p. 148** © Cartoonresource/Shutterstock ; **p. 151** *1* © Kositlimsiri/ Shutterstock ; *2* © Robert Biedermann/Shutterstock ; **p. 154** © DR ; **p. 157** © Tim Graham/Alamy Stock Photo/Photo12 ; **p. 161** © Manoj Verma/Hindustan Times/Getty Images ; **p. 163** © Kositlimsiri/Shutterstock ; **p. 165** © Alexandre Dupeyron ; **p. 168** © Indranil Mukherjee/Afp ; **p. 175** *1* © Khvost/Shutterstock ; *2* © Tarzhanova/Shutterstock ; *3* © Africa Studio/Shutterstock ; *4* © elenovsky/Shutterstock ; *5* © ronstik/Shutterstock ; *6* © Jiang Hongyan/Shutterstock ; *7* © Andrii Gorulko/Shutterstock ; *8* © Valentyn Volkov/Shutterstock ; *9* © Tim UR/Shutterstock ; *10* © johnfoto18/Shutterstock ; **p. 176** *1* © Martin Good/Shutterstock ; *2* © Songquan Deng/Shutterstock ; *3* © Songquan Deng/Shutterstock ; *4* © Dima Sid/Shutterstock ; *5* © canadastock/Shutterstock ; *6* © ARENA Creative/Shutterstock ; *7* © arbit/Shutterstock ; *8* © Olga1818/Shutterstock.

Références textes

p. 37 nytimes.com/DR ; **p. 39** change4lifewales.org.uk/DR ; **p. 56** thehighline.org/DR ; **p. 66** shortstoriesshort.com/DR ; **p. 77** © Roald Dahl, Little Red Riding Hood and the Wolf, ed. Jonathan Cape, 1982 ; **p. 81** © Roald Dahl, Little Red Riding Hood and the Wolf, ed. Jonathan Cape, 1982 ; **p. 108** timeforkids.com/DR ; **p. 113** westminsterinternationalshop.com/ DR ; **p. 117** bbc.co.uk/DR ; **p. 144** visithoustontexas.com/DR ; **p. 155** bkbirlacentre.com/DR ; **p. 161** mumbaitheatreguide.com/DR ; **p. 162** timesofindia.indiatimes.com/DR ;

Achevé d'imprimer en Italie par L.E.G.O. S.p.A, Lavis - Dépôt légal : Mars 2017 - Édition 01 - Collection 06 - 96/6602/9